Praise for Quail Bell

"The third issue of Quail Bell, from Richmond, Virginia, also contains numerous short essays, here focusing on Baltimore and Washington, DC. One particularly memorable work looks at the DC neighborhood of Anacostia, gentrification, and the current state of DC's Old Town; another goes inside offbeat spaces in Baltimore. There's some humor as well — for whatever reason, Victorian street urchin humor is a sort of comedic gift that keeps on giving. And there's a good-sized visual arts component here, too, from a collection of drawings to some beautiful photos of a small town near Guadalajara, to an interview with photographer Alexander C. Kafka. In the end, Quail Bell felt like the record of a tightly-knit community; time will tell what else emerges."

–Tobias Carroll, Vol. 1 *Brooklyn*

"[The second issue of] Quail Bell is a lovely, perfect-bound publication helmed by Christine Stoddard that features a mixture of fiction, essay, and memoir writing, side by side with grayscale art. Deceptively beautiful in its presentation, there's a dark subversiveness that runs through the content with discussions on Countess Bathory, Greek sex practices and haunted cities. It's a capital-R Romantic vision brought to print, and one that's well worth seeking out."

–Tenebrous Kate, *Love Train for the Tenebrous Empire*

THE NEST

An Anthology of The Unreal
BY QUAIL BELL MAGAZINE

Featuring Stories from 2010-2012

Compiled by Jade Miller

BELLE ISLE BOOKS

ISBN 978-1-9399300-9-5
LCCN 2013949736

Edited by Jade Miller, Julie DiNisio, and Christine Stoddard
Designed by Kristen Rebelo
Thanks to Sean Marks

Quail Bell Magazine
P. O. Box 4844
Richmond, Virginia 23220
www.quailbellmagazine.com

Published by

BELLE ISLE BOOKS
www.belleislebooks.com

We dedicate this book to all of our favorite fledglings—the ones who adore the imaginary, the nostalgic, and the otherworldly as much as we do.

~ The Quail Bell Crew

TABLE OF CONTENTS

FOREWORD

Dear fledglings,

Thank you for picking up *Quail Bell Magazine*'s inaugural book project (whether you actually bought it or are just flipping through it in the back of the bookstore.). This anthology originated as a single book filled with The Quail Bell Crew's' favorite pieces that have run on our online magazine over the past couple of years. But sometimes you lay one egg and two chicks come out. That situation emerged here, too.

When I first started *Quail Bell Magazine* as a small, personal blog in 2010, The Real vs. The Unreal was one of its key features and remain so today, though the two categories eventually evolved into separate blogs on the site. Readers and contributors often tell me that this element of the website's design is what initially piqued their interest—and kept them coming back. Naturally, when Jade Miller, Julie DiNisio, and I set down to edit this book, we had to honor the Quail Bell tradition of experimentation. And thus we toyed and ultimately settled upon cobbling together two anthologies that explore the real and unreal aspects of "the imaginary, the nostalgic, and the otherworldly."

Whether you're holding *Airborne* (The Real) or *The Nest* (The Unreal), I hope you'll have a chance to check out the companion anthology, as well. If you're not already familiar with *Quail Bell Magazine*—a website dedicated to the arts, literature, history, folklore, and other oddities—please hop on over to www.quailbellmagazine.com. We update the website daily and also print a quarterly just for the heck of it. Because what's better than pixels? Paper!

Here's a toast to words and letters and dreams. They've been the stuff of *Quail Bell*'s magic since the very beginning, and hopefully will continue to be, far into the future. Thanks to our loyal readers for all the love, generosity, and, of course, page views.

Feathery hugs,

Christine Stoddard, August 2013
Founder and Editor
Quail Bell Magazine
www.quailbellmagazine.com

SHEDDING LIGHT

BY MICHAEL C. KEITH

T
he cemetery is an open space among the ruins . . .
—Percy Bysshe Shelley

Margaret Hamlin lived across the street from a small, centuries-old cemetery. Its neglected appearance had disturbed her since she moved into her house. In the beginning she tried to avoid looking at the burial ground but found that was impossible, since her large bay window faced it. Keeping the drapes closed only made the living room in her house dreary during the day, and she found the idea of having to turn on the lights before nightfall depressing.

Eventually she decided on a solution to the problem—she would spruce up the graveyard. She began to pull the weeds surrounding the headstones and to plant colorful flowers in a few strategic spots.

Despite her efforts, the cemetery remained a gloomy and forlorn patch of land for half of the year, given the frigid northern Wisconsin winters. The cold gave it a bareness that accentuated the leaning and decrepit monuments and made Margaret all the more mindful of the ancient remains beneath them. In the twilight shadows, the headstones took on an even more disturbing aspect. The slightest unevenness of the ground became a swollen bulge, as though something were pushing up against the cool earth, attempting to escape. To Margaret, it was easy to imagine that the dead were being unearthed, propelled upward by a profound sadness.

So Margaret decided to take further action. She would add lights, colored lights, in an attempt to improve the bleak aura that hung over the resting place of people who had likely once lived on the very land where her house now sat.

Why do graveyards have to be such lonely, foreboding places? she wondered on her way to the local hardware store. *Didn't the deceased once revel in the joys of life? Why are they depicted in such melancholy and grim terms? We die, but does it change who we were? We no longer breathe, but does that turn us into something terrible . . . monsters?*

"I hate those horror movies. Zombies . . . my word," she grumbled as she pulled into Ryerson's Variety Emporium, more determined than ever to give the old graveyard a face-lift.

In short order, Margaret found strings of tinted bulbs and spotlights. But how would she power them so far away from her house?

"Could probably use a heavy duty extension cord," said the young clerk. "We got a hundred-footer. You could connect a couple of them if you need real length. Cars will just roll over them. Shouldn't cause a disconnection. What are you using them for?"

"Oh, just want to decorate something across from my house," answered Margaret, evasively.

"Well, all these pretty lights should do the trick."

"I hope so," said Margaret, paying for her goods. "If not, I'll be back for more."

• • •

The next morning, Margaret unraveled the long extension cords and, to her great satisfaction, found that they reached the cemetery with room to spare. She then draped the colored lights over several tombstones and arranged two spotlights so they would splash their glow over the lot.

When evening arrived, she excitedly hit the switch, and, to her delight, what had been a dreary chasm was transformed into a luminous tableau.

"Oh my. How wonderful. That's how it should be. Not a place of gloom and doom, for heaven's sake."

The few cars that typically used the road slowed as they passed the illuminated resting place. Each subsequent evening, more cars appeared, and some pulled to a stop to take in the full effect. One driver parked his car and followed the extension cord to Margaret's house to express his satisfaction with her handiwork.

"Never did see a cemetery all lit up like that. It sure does make you feel better about those sad places," he said with a broad smile that brought one to Margaret's face.

That night, Margaret decided to add more lights to brighten some of the monuments at the far reaches of the graveyard. No reason anyone should be neglected, she thought, feeling happier than she had in a long time. Life had mostly been a burden to Margaret since her retirement and divorce. It had been ages since she experienced a sense of purpose, and illuminating the graveyard gave her one.

• • •

News of her deed spread, and one Tuesday morning, she found herself the subject of an interview in the local newspaper. The reporter, Deek Bellows, asked what motivated Margaret to decorate the cemetery, and she enthusiastically gave a full account.

"Well, it does make sense that the living should make an effort to improve the resting places of the departed. They sure can be pretty dreary," observed Bellows, who then posed another question. "Do you know there's a pretty notorious character buried there?"

"No, I didn't. Who might that be?"

"Seymour Crowley. Killed his wife and daughter and then took his own life. They're buried there with him up in back, I think. Apparently he acted out of fear that his family had smallpox. Really was chicken pox though. A terrible tragedy. Names are pretty much worn off their headstones, but some old folk around here still know the story of Crazy Crowley, as he came to be called. Come to think of it, they may not take too kindly to your prettying up the place or drawing attention to it. Was a pretty big shock and embarrassment to the town when it happened all those years ago. You can imagine."

Margaret lifted a hand to her cheek, feeling her skin flush beneath her fingertips. "Oh my," she murmured, "I had no idea."

The reporter left her feeling somewhat conflicted about her work on the graveyard, but as she fixed herself a turkey sandwich for lunch, she came to the conclusion that it didn't matter that one of its occupants had committed murder. What was important to Margaret was that he had done so thinking he was sparing his family the pain of a horrible disease. In her mind, the act had even been heroic. It soon became apparent to Margaret that others didn't feel that way. She'd just finished washing her lunch dishes when the doorbell rang.

"Hello, Mrs. Hamlin. I'm here to ask you to remove those lights from the cemetery," said a middle-aged man in coveralls.

"Well, why should I do that?" inquired Margaret, blocking the entrance to her house.

"'Cause it ain't right. That's why."

"What isn't right?"

"To be making something of that wicked place," grumbled the man.

"Wicked? What's so wicked about a little graveyard?"

"Crazy Crowley's buried there, and he murdered his kin."

"And how do you know that?" asked Margaret, beginning to feel her blood rise.

"He was my great uncle twice removed. Gave my ancestors nothing but heartbreak with what he done. My mama heard about you prettying up his grave and she near fainted. Had me come over here to get you to stop."

"Look, Mr. . . . ?"

"Crowley. Just like . . . like him" said the man, pointing in the direction of the cemetery. "I'm Edward, though."

"Mr. Crowley . . . Edward," Margaret proceeded, "there are other people buried there, too. Besides, what your relative did wasn't without compassion. He thought his family was dying from smallpox and didn't want them to suffer. It was a terrible misunderstanding."

"Maybe so, but he killed them just the same and gave the Crowley name a bad reputation. We don't need to remind people of that by your making a carnival of the place."

"I'm doing no such thing. I'm just trying to make it . . . well, less gloomy," defended Margaret.

"That's what it's supposed to be. Dead people are there. It's not an amusement park, for mercy's sake. Just get them blasted lights out of there. Besides, ain't your kin buried there. You only been here for a while and want to change things that ain't your business."

The man turned and quickly strode to his parked pickup truck. Margaret was tempted to call after him that she had no intention of removing the lights, but she kept quiet. When he sped away, she gave her door a good hard slam.

"The audacity," she mumbled, pouring herself a rare third cup of coffee.

• • •

For the balance of the day, she fumed over the encounter, and when nightfall came, it gratified her to turn on the cemetery lights. *Revenge is sweet*, she told herself.

"There you go, folks. Enjoy the deserved attention," said Margaret, with uncharacteristic bravado.

She turned off the living room lamp and dragged a chair over to the bay window. There she sat, observing the cars as they meandered by the cemetery. By the time she was ready to go to bed, she calculated that the number of cars passing her house had doubled since the day she first brightened up the burial ground. It filled her with pride that her effort was causing people to have more appreciation for the resting place of the long departed.

Poor forgotten souls . . . no one should ever be ignored because they're gone, thought Margaret, finally going to bed and quickly slipping into a deep, satisfying sleep. It was past eight when she woke up, and the sunlight in the room caused her to squint as she reached for her robe.

The cemetery lights, she recalled, *I need to turn them off.* As she looked out of her second-floor bedroom window, Margaret noticed an object on her lawn but could not make it out. *I need new glasses. Better make an appointment with the eye doctor.* From her living room window, she was able to identify what sat in front of her house. *What the . . . ?* The strings of colored lights, spotlights, and extension cords were neatly stacked next to the birdbath. It immediately occurred to Margaret that Edward Crowley had taken action into his own hands. *Well, that's not going to happen, fella.* After she downed a cup of coffee, she returned the lights to their original location, vowing to stay awake that night to confront Crowley if he returned.

As soon as the late day sun fell behind the pine trees, Margaret hit the switch to light the graveyard. She sat at the bay window and poured herself a hot cup of cocoa from the thermos she had filled in anticipation of a long night. Cars soon began to appear on the street. At one point, she counted seven vehicles parked in front of the cemetery, and again she felt great satisfaction. It was well after midnight when the last car left the site, and despite filling herself with caffeine, Margaret had to fight to remain awake and ultimately lost the battle. She awoke as dawn was breaking.

"Shoot!" she blurted, again finding the cemetery lighting coiled up on her lawn.

She dressed quickly and reconnected the lights to the graveyard. She then located Edward Crowley's address in the phone book and drove to his house. A woman who Margaret assumed was his wife answered the door and, without hesitation, invited her inside. Mrs. Crowley called for her husband, who immediately emerged from the kitchen.

"Can I help you, Mrs. Hamlin?" said Crowley with a sour look.

"Yes, indeed, you can, Mr. Crowley. I would greatly appreciate it if you would stop removing the lights from the cemetery. You know why I put them there, and although you have your reasons for not liking them, everyone else in town seems to appreciate them."

"I don't know what you're talking about. I haven't done nothing like that," protested Crowley, with a sincerity that surprised her and made her doubt her conviction.

"Well, if you didn't, who did?"

"Maybe someone else don't like all the attention you're bringing to that old bone yard. But I can tell you it ain't me pulling them lights off. I got better things to do with my time, like getting to work right now," said Crowley, turning his back on Margaret and disappearing from the room.

"Is there anything else I can do for you?" asked Mrs. Crowley sweetly.

"No, sorry to bother you," replied Margaret, feeling awkward.

If he didn't do it, who did? wondered Margaret on her drive home. *Probably some kids pulling a prank.*

● ● ●

That evening the largest crowd ever gathered at the graveyard. The visitors were mostly teenagers and left their cars to romp through the headstones with music blaring from a boom box. The partying went on until late at night, and Margaret was tempted to confront the revelers but resisted the urge to do so, fearing the consequences.

"So disrespectful," Margaret mumbled, finally climbing into bed after things had quieted down.

Not long after she had drifted off, a loud crash caused her to bolt upright in bed. Glass from the shattered window covered her bedspread. At the foot of the bed was one of the graveyard spotlights. Margaret pushed the covers aside and walked carefully to the broken window. What she saw outside caused her to gasp. *It can't be! Impossible!* Standing under her bedroom window was a decomposed figure in a rotted waistcoat.

"LET US REST IN PEACE!" bellowed the reanimated corpse, which turned and lurched back toward the cemetery.

"Crazy Crowley, is that you?" shouted Margaret, causing the cadaver to stop and glance back at her malevolently.

It then vanished into the darkness.

"Well, be that way," grumbled Margaret indignantly.

As she expected, she found the cemetery lights on her lawn when morning arrived. Instead of restoring them yet again, she put them in the garage.

"You try to do something nice, and this is what you get . . . ," she huffed.

Margaret returned to her house and closed the curtains in her living room. They stayed that way for some years, until one day, the time came for her to occupy a forgotten plot of earth.

THE PEOPLE WHO LIVE IN MY BEARD

BY NEVILLE TURNER

I can't be too sure, but I'm beginning to suspect that there are people living in my beard. They moved in a while ago, setting up camp in the woods at the end of my chin.

They're not normal sized people, obviously. They're tiny ones, with heads the size of peanuts, limbs thinner than matchsticks, and sesame seed eyes. Sometimes when I'm watching TV, I can see them in my peripheral vision, but as soon as I look down, they're gone. I keep trying anyway.

I used to think it was all in my head, but then I started to find evidence: tiny clothes, leftover food, and small shelters woven from the shorter hairs. Initially I was creeped out, but I'm starting to like them. How many people can say they've got their own little community contained within their beard?

If I pretend to be asleep, I can hear them talking. I can't make out what they say, though; their voices are so small and gentle, like whispers that tickle the tiny bones hidden within your ears. Sometimes it tickles so much, I can't contain the giggles. As soon as I let it out though, they go quiet. They're a very secretive bunch. I've tried talking to them, but they never talk back.

They've been with me for almost a year now; they moved in when she moved out.

THE DEAD RIVER

BY ERIN COLE

Where there is a dead river, there is a wilting echo in time, a parched memory frayed and thinned in the helix of life. All that thrived has dried and vanished, but the fish will return. The larvae will reclaim sustenance to convert gelatinous bodies into fluttering, gossamer and black velvet wings, and sunlight will find a fractured path down the clear, jade run once again. There will be no more blood, no more sinew and muscle folding over sand and rock—just bones, camouflaged within the rocky banks of crusted clay and lime.

● ● ●

"Green Lady?"

The Lady of the Forest lifted her head from a corner of foliage. "Yes?" It was Little Fawn again. So new to and unsure of his world, she thought. She nestled her head back under a fern and counted the striated rows of spores that laced the edges.

"There is a ruckus of a flock down at the Dead River."

Flock meant only one thing—Raven and her clan. "Did Raven send for me?"

Little Fawn nibbled on tender shoots of wild yarrow stretching from a blanket of rot. "No, but the girl did."

"Girl?" The Lady's brow creased into a blade of grass.

"Yes, down at the Dead River."

The Lady of the Forest stood, tuning her senses past a symphony of June bugs that snapped like summer fire in the hollowed-out trunks of cedar and pine. There, in the soft emerald air of the hills, a whisper drifted.

Why had she not heard it until now? She heard every call, knew of every misplaced spirit, answered to all cries as do the elephants of the prairie.

Little Fawn sensed her thoughts. "It is difficult to concentrate with so many requests, Lady of the Forest."

"No, Little Fawn. It is something else, another reason."

The Lady of the Forest slid from a bed of liverwort and traveled through the dark of the forest toward the Dead River. Little Fawn skipped and bounded close behind her, stumbling across slippery logs and earth-covered boulders. Brush rustled with foxes and chipmunks, and beneath the needles, the night crawlers slithered, foraging organics from sodden dirt.

The Lady of the Forest sensed a season of change was approaching, not unlike the feeling that the first crisp chill of dawn stirred in her each year. Fall was afoot, but it went deeper than that. There was an ebbing of her spirit—not so much a weakening as it was a turning inward, a need for dormancy. She felt it in the rigidity of her step and the languor of her reflections, but to question if her disconnection might be to blame for the girl's lost spirit settled shadows across her soul.

A cool breeze stirred the Lady's attention. The Air Maiden wields a delicate power. She is a portable vessel of scent, seed, and sound, and she can be an ominous fury of unseen force. Tonight, she wound between the trunks of the forest reverberating with yesterday's wails.

A gust of wind whipped beside the Lady of the Forest: Air Maiden's whisper. "She called for you. Listen—"

Bitter as regret in the Lady's heart, the girl's cry ricocheted from mountain to shore. It crested like an icy tide against the Lady's heart, and she ducked against the coldness of truth, determined to persevere through her journey.

Another gust curled around the Lady: "She said you were cruel and heartless."

"She doesn't understand," the Lady replied.

Worry tainted the Air Maiden's question with a cold bite. "How will you help her now?"

That the Lady did not know, and she wondered if she even could.

Little Fawn dipped into a valley to escape the Air Maiden's icy current. The Lady of the Forest followed. He paused at the crackling of twigs and turned his head to the side.

Mother Bear's shadow was a hollow darkness through the trees. Two specks of light from her eyes centered on Little Fawn. He stilled with fear racing beneath his hide, hoping to achieve invisibility through his inert silence.

"Back up, Little Fawn," the Lady of the Forest whispered.

But Little Fawn had to learn on his own. He searched the blackness beyond Mother Bear, perceived safety, and cut past her left side. She disliked Little Fawn's rapid movement and his proximity to her nearby young. Her claws stretched out, raking the backside of Little Fawn. He twisted under her strength and continued bounding toward deep shadows.

The stench of blood surrounding Mother Bear assured Lady of the Forest that she was too gorged and fatigued to bother with Little Fawn, and she and her cubs rumbled back to a warm, dry den. The Lady of the Forest moved on, the foreign sense of urgency quickening her pace. The flora of the forest blinked and stared.

Green Man keeps a watchful gaze. His heart a verdant cauldron of life, his eyes as sharp as a hawk's, he guards the wildlife of the forest with fierce devotion. He shuddered branches in front of the Lady.

"The girl was here, circling around for days," he groaned. "She tore at limbs and shrubs and disrupted the animals. She could not change her outcome."

"Change is . . ." *difficult to undertake when forced upon us*, the Lady thought. "Change can be premature."

The crown of a hemlock bowed toward the Lady. "And where were you, Green Lady? What of your nature?"

To deny her state was of no use. "My nature is wrought with obstacles, but you know as well as I do that the spiral of the universe will continue its endless voyage."

"Even the girl's?"

"Yes. The girl's too."

Green Man lifted his eyes from the Lady and allowed her passage through a dense grove.

The Lady of the Forest came into a clearing, the valley of the Dead River. Fallen trunks crisscrossed an arid canyon, and boulders were stacked precariously without regard for gravity.

It was here that Air Maiden called home. The canyon was a natural, melodic hallway, and the border of evergreens danced in her breeze.

The Lady of the Forest inhaled deeply. Along with Air Maiden's harmonics, she also brought the scent of death—putrid, sweet, and sour. The Lady knew then that she was close.

Moonlight slipped through the branches and shone upon a trail of a thousand carnivorous ants and beetles. The Lady noted their direction: south, toward the bottom of the Dead River. Their journey would lead to sustenance. Death.

Little Fawn caught up with the Lady and licked at the gash in his pelt.

She knew he would heal well, so she continued through the canyon. It wasn't long before the Lady of the Forest and Little Fawn found the ruckus of animals circled around a bend in the Dead River.

There, tucked in the elbow of a birch, the girl's body lay. Concave flesh decayed, withered into wood and stone, and her cavities were splayed to the hunger of others. In the ugliness of her death, she was nonetheless as brilliant as the reddest of roses. So absolute was her beauty that even non-scavengers gathered in her presence, to bask in the mysterious splendor of the cadaver.

"She will not let us eat," Raven spat when the Lady of the Forest approached.

Another black bird, smaller, but just as brave, cawed. "We're starving, and the flies are embedding their eggs into the best parts!"

A gray shadow flitted near the base of a stump. It was the lingering echo of the girl. Her clothes were soiled and torn, and her dark hair was long and matted. Her eyes had sunken in, as if empty.

She straightened and marched toward the Lady of the Forest. "You did this!" she shouted at her. "You made me lost! I was so cold, delirious, and desperate that I couldn't find my way out!" Sobs overcame her.

The yelling scared Little Fawn, and he crouched behind the Lady. Raven and her clan hopped onto a stiff elbow and jerked at exposed flesh. The girl picked up a handful of rocks and threw them at the scavengers, shooing them away from her body.

"Get out of here!" She lunged at them, waving her thin arms.

The birds squawked and drummed black wings into the air. Forlorn, the girl slumped back to the ground, holding her hands up to cover her face.

The Lady of the Forest wanted to hold her, tell her that there was more to life than the one she knew, that life was woven of many threads.

Collected in the hollow of a boulder, a small pool of water reflected the dim radiance of the stars and moon above. The Lady leaned over it. Lines had deepened into her face, grooved like the bark of trees. The time for change had come. It wasn't until that moment that the Lady remembered: even answers had their own clock.

"I didn't hear you, my child, for I wasn't supposed to."

The girl looked up. "I don't understand."

The Lady turned to Little Fawn and wiped her weathered hand across his back, scooping his white spots into a palm-full of ivory petals. He was too old for them now.

The Lady of the Forest walked over to the girl. "In the helix of life, we cannot remain constant. Adaptation is in our nature, and the more we oppose the cycles of the cosmos, the further we recede from our destiny."

The Lady of the Forest blew the petals like children's bubbles over the girl's body. At their touch, a lucent essence lifted from the remains. Sheer as a dragonfly's wing, it crossed into the shadow of the lost girl.

She stopped crying and stood. Brightness filled her eyes. She reached for the Lady, who clasped her hands in her own.

There was a moment of recognition between the Girl of the Woods and the Lady of the Forest. The Girl understood that life was a continuous cycle—birth, death, and rebirth. The Lady realized that each twist in the helix brought fear and uncertainty, neither of which was ever permanent.

"Thank you, my Lady," the Girl of the Woods said.

The Lady of the Forest smiled and let go of the Girl's hands. Then her arms lengthened and twisted into timber. Roots protruded from her feet and burrowed into the ground. Her hair molded into weeping bows of pine and needle, ears and nose into cones, and her crown soared upward, aspiring for the eye of Andromeda in the ocean of night above.

Little Fawn scratched his back against the Lady's trunk, nudging tender spots at the top of his head where bone was pushing through. The Girl of the Woods gazed around the forest, knowing that she, too, would discover its secrets, just as the Lady of the Forest had before her.

She pulled herself up onto a branch of the Lady Redwood. Swinging her bare feet from a mossy perch, the Girl of the Woods listened to a cricket lullaby and watched the universe turn.

SHADOWS

BY ALEXANDER C. KAFKA

S hadows stalk me still.
Never get their fill.
How could you delight
in the morning's light
if the nighttime had no will?

When the evening comes,
our contents under pressure,
antiseptic, screwed on tight,
strictly contained—

will you meet my eyes
and read their urgent message
and confront your demons
when I call your name?

Rock me tender, rock me slow.
There's still time till you must go.
Even if it's just one night,
kiss me long and hold me tight.
Rock me tender, rock me slow.

Long as you're alone,
as your desires roam,
smile as you may,
however bright the day,
you'll face shadows of your own.

Let our palettes merge,
our shadows, light converge
into a panorama rich
as it is bold.

Let the shadows play
and make their cautious way
amid the cool of living's shades
and feeling's folds.

Rock me tender, rock me slow.
Must you leave? Why must you go?
Let the day carry the night.
Kiss me long and hold me tight.
Rock me tender, rock me slow.

BREATHE

BY CALEB TRUE

A long time ago, in a time before time, before thought and wish, want, or need, the Creator-Spirit sent four humans to the earth and charged them to find out what it was they should breathe.

"There are four elements, my children," said the Creator-Spirit. "Earth, fire, water, and air. There are four directions to this world and four of you. Pick a substance and pick a direction, and discover what it is that humans should breathe."

And so the four people chose their elements and their directions, said their good-byes, and departed.

The first human headed east, and after a long time walking found himself at the lip of a great desert. The first human was terrified by the desert's vastness. He swallowed his fear, continued on, but the sun beat down on him ferociously, scorching his back and drying his eyes. The first human remembered the charge given him by the Creator-Spirit, and thought, "If I breathed earth, I could travel underground and be hidden from this furious sun."

And the man fell to his knees and began to dig with his hands. He dug and dug, filling his fingernails with grit, but the depression he was making kept on filling back up with loose sand.

Eventually, his furious digging revealed a mole rat, blind and pink and indignant.

"Man-father, what are you doing, ruining my home?" croaked the mole rat.

"Mole rat," said the human, "I did not know, I am sorry."

"What do you think you are doing, digging in the sand?" asked the mole rat.

"I thought if I could travel in the earth as you do, I could avoid the burning sun, as you do."

"Burning sun!" scoffed the mole rat. "Look at your skin, it is thick and tawny. It can withstand the sun. Look at my skin," said the mole rat, and the first human did. "You see?" said the mole rat. "Now look at my paws. The underground is my home, man-father. Leave it be. You must take refuge from the beating sun elsewhere."

The first human plodded on.

With the sun now sinking below the horizon behind him, the first human now feared he might die in this wasteland. The stars came out, the breeze picked up, and the man began to shiver. He cried as he walked, hugging himself, but then he tripped over a small stone, and landed spread-eagled on the ground. The sand warmed him, and the man said, "If only I can bury myself in this sand, I can survive the cold desert night and continue another day." And the man lay down on the warm sand and, instead of digging, scooped handfuls of sand over him, over and over, until he was cozy warm and covered. For a moment, only the man's face peeked out of the sand, facing the stars above, and he thanked his Creator-Spirit for bringing him wisdom. Then with one last scoop, the man covered his face with warm sand and fell asleep to the music of shifting sands in the night.

The second human headed south, confident in herself, knowing she would be the one who would answer her Creator-Spirit's wish. She walked for a long time, her spirits never waning, when she caught the smell of something acrid in the distance. Sensing death and seeing a black blotch on the horizon, she froze for a moment, then gritted her teeth and continued on. As she traversed the curve of the earth, she discovered a great forest fire. Deer charged out of the wood with drowning eyes and foaming mouths; groups of crows escaped in all directions. The second human watched them retreat as she walked toward the trees and the bubble of heat. The fire crackled and branches snapped. Great trunks groaned and came crashing to the ground, sending up gouts of smoke and sparks.

The second human stopped at the lip of the flame and inhaled deeply. The hot air stung her throat, tickled it in such a way that she doubled over coughing. A beaver, having just escaped the lick of flame by the skin of his two teeth, let out a rasping laugh.

"Man-mother," said the beaver, "you cannot hope to breathe smoke and sparks! Are you trying to die?"

The second human stood and regarded the beaver, gently massaging her clavicle with one hand. "Of course not, Beaver," she said. "What would you have me do?"

"Man-mother," said the beaver, "I have just escaped suffocation by the skin of my two teeth. I crawl on four feet, I run like I haven't a burdensome and clumsy tail, I rub all the world with my fat belly in my desire to stay low and avoid breathing the smoke and choking sparks!"

As the beaver and the second human conversed, time passed, and the sun, tired of the day, retreated toward the western horizon. It winked at last to the second human, to the beaver, and then disappeared. The fire in the forest had diminished to a bright heart of undying ember at the center of the wood. The heavens glowed a strange purple. No stars came out.

"Well, man-mother," said the beaver, "it is now night, though a reluctant one, I must say, and I must go find a home."

The breeze picked up, and the second human closed her arms around herself for warmth. "Can I come with you?" said the second human. "I haven't a home."

"Man-mother," said the beaver, "I don't know where home is! My old home was consumed by the great fire! First, I must find a home, and then, I fear, it would still be inadequate for you: too small, too squalid, too many pointy places to prick your exposed flesh while you sleep, and too cold."

The second human let her hands fall to her sides dejectedly, and nodded. "All right, Beaver," she said, "good night to you."

"Good night, man-mother," said the beaver as he left.

As night deepened, the second human's spirits dimmed. She inched her way deeper into the steaming wood for warmth, finding the forest floor ever warmer underfoot. Cinders crunched beneath her, warm coals made the woods themselves shimmer. After a long time trekking toward the heart of the fire, the human grew dizzy from the haze, and she reached out to the nearest tree trunk for support. Her hand entered the trunk easily, and she withdrew a fistful of ash. The tree collapsed beside her and she covered her mouth and turned away from the billow. A sheer wind cut through the trees and chilled her for a moment. Growing desperate, she pressed on, seeking a place with enough living fire to keep her warm through the night. After hours of searching, she collapsed into a little heap, displacing a cloud of ash, and lamented: "Creator-Spirit, what am I to do? I cannot seem to get close enough to fire even to warm my bones! It is so late, and I am so tired, what can I do to preserve my body?"

Just then a secret compartment of oxygen exposed itself from beneath a blanket of insulating peat—a beaver's burrow, no doubt—and fire gulped it up greedily. The second human jumped when a pillar of flamed erupted just a few feet from her.

The second human hungered for warmth, hungered to take the hot core inside her and be warmed from the inside out. The thought thrilled her, even sparked a spontaneous knot of something warm-like deep within her, and it was from this sensation that she knew her instincts were right. She exhaled deeply, then stepped into the pillar of fire.

The third human trekked west, resolving not to stop until he came to a vast ocean. He walked and walked, and stopped a few times, considering his options. He stopped for the first time at a lake. He tested the water, stepping in. The muddy bank swallowed his feet. He took another step, pulling his feet out of the suck and replacing them again, then stopped. A water snake glided over to where he stood, filthy, glued to the shallows, sinking.

"Man-father," said the water snake, "what in the name of the Creator-Spirit are you doing?"

"I am trying to find out what it is that humans should breathe. I am to breathe this lake in," said the third human.

The water snake nodded. "Yes, admirable. But stupid," said the water snake.

"Mind your own business, Water Snake," said the third human.

"You'd be wise to listen to what I have to say and to appreciate the fact that I haven't kissed you full of venom yet," said the water snake. "I confess, I lust to."

The third human swallowed and cupped his hands around his penis, embarrassed. "What have you got to say, Water Snake?"

"This lake is useless to you. The mud is deeper than the lake at all points."

"Even in the center of the lake?' asked the third human. As he spoke, he sank slowly, the mud drinking him in little by little.

"Even in the center," said the water snake. "And if you continue to stand there asking man-questions, you will soon be breathing mud!"

The man flailed for a moment, losing his balance, realizing he was up to his thighs in muck, up to his penis in water. "What should I do?" asked the man, panicking.

"Lie back, and let me kiss you," said the water snake.

"But I'll die from your kiss," said the third human.

"I won't, I promise. I will resist," said the water snake, and to prove he was no liar, unhinged his jaw to show just how he'd kiss without releasing poison. "Just a peck," hissed the snake, getting ready, "to save your life. No venom."

The third human lay back, the snake kissed him good on the shoulder, and dragged him to a safe place ashore where the ground was hard. The third human trekked on.

Finally, he arrived at the ocean just as the sun was setting. The scene was beautiful. The third human wept as he cleaned his snakebitten shoulder with saltwater, and the sun disappeared behind the horizon. The stars came out, the wind grew cold all around him, and he knew there was only one place left to go.

The fourth human headed north, seeking a fresh air to breath. At first she could smell only the smoke from a distant forest fire, and she covered her mouth with a cupped hand. She walked and walked, and as she progressed northward, the temperature grew colder around her. Eventually, with the sun hanging in the western sky to her left, the fourth human flagged down a flying V of geese.

"Ho," she called. "Geese!"

And one goose craned its limber neck to see what was the matter. It saw the fourth human and gestured for the others to circle around. They alighted, still in V formation on the ground, before fourth human.

"Geese," she said, "where can I find the purest air? I am on a quest for the Creator-Spirit."

"The purest air?" asked the lead goose. "What do you mean, purest?"

"The youngest air," chimed in a second goose.

"The air most ignorant!" chimed in a third goose.

"The air unfouled!" chimed in a fourth goose, and—

"Unfowled?" quipped a fifth, "I hope not. But we cannot possibly know of such an air, being ourselves fowlers!"

The rest of the V honked in laughter.

"The cleanest air," said the fourth human, "that I might breathe."

And they all trilled, "Ohhhh," then said, "Follow us." And the fourth human did.

She followed the geese into the darkness of the night till she could barely make out their dark forms against a purple sky. The stars came out, backlighting the silhouetted birds. At last, they came to a resting spot. The flapping geese alighted on a outcropping of rocks. The fourth human shivered, teeth chattering, breasts goose-pimpled, stopping behind them. "Here?" she asked.

"Here!" said the lead goose. "Here shall we hibernate, procreate, recreate!"

The fourth human looked around, shocked by the austerity of the landscape. It was flat and shone white in the starlight. A blighted place.

"Is this spot not adequate, man-mother?" asked the lead goose.

Another goose waddled up. "Is the air not fresh?"

The fourth human inhaled a short breath, but the icy cold of the air stung her lungs and she doubled over, coughing. The geese honked in laughter again at her, fluttering their wings. "Never satisfied," they honked, "never satisfied, this man-mother, this child of the Creator-Spirit."

And so the fourth human marched on.

But the first human did not drown in the sand . . .

He awoke the next day in a dark mole rat's tunnel, roughly the shape and size of his body, out of which he eventually crawled, following sunlight to the surface of the earth. And he trekked on, seeking an earth he could adequately drink. He found mud, and spat it out for the water—not his quest. He found rich soil, but refused to breathe in a worm, an insect, an oak tree's massive root system. He walked onward, circumnavigating the whole world over until he found himself standing, dumbstruck, in the very spot where he'd left the Creator-Spirit.

And the second human did not dissolve into flames . . .

She stepped into the fire, yes, but the oxygen greedily sucked from the beaver's burrow was drunk all too quickly, and when the second human placed a foot in the flames, she stamped them out. She was utterly disappointed. She plodded on, traversing the smoldering woods to their terminus and continuing on beyond that, beyond the horizon, traversing the whole world over, till she found herself standing in the spot where she'd left the Creator-Spirit.

And the third human, he did not drink in all the oceans and become a permanent fixture of the bottom of the sea . . .

He could not sink. He could drink, and drink, but soon found himself sick from seawater, and still readily buoyant—the sea would not take him. He tried to breathe in the sea, but his body reacted violently and he decided, then and there, that indeed man had not been intended to breathe the oceans of the world. The third human floated, and floated, and the sun came up, and went down again, and after many days he drifted off to sleep, not waking until he was washed up on a distant shore. He stood and continued, as he was charged, westward, and found himself standing in the spot where he'd left the Creator-Spirit long before. He had news for the Creator-Spirit, news he would deliver soberly and matter-of-factly. But the Creator-Spirit did not come.

Instead came the fourth human.

She never did find a pure air to breathe—not too hot, not too cold, not too smoky.

The fourth human trekked the whole world over, disappointed by the relative iciness, humid soupiness, or buffeting dryness of the earth's many winds. She, like the others, wound up in the spot where she'd left the Creator-Spirit.

The third human saw her, the fourth, approach out of the south, having rounded the whole of the globe, naked, with a determined look on her face, so beautiful and exposed and human. So full of utility. The third human felt himself welling up inside and discovered that he had let some seed, had become wet like the ocean he'd tried so sincerely to drink.

The fourth human saw the third human, standing and seeming to welcome her back from what had felt like an interminable stroll. She felt excitement and gratitude grip her heart. It beat faster and faster, and her breath shortened, till it seemed she was struggling for air.

The second human found herself moving towards the origin, knowing where she was because of the familiar surroundings. She noticed the third and fourth humans also approaching, from exact angles, from a distance, but with such intensity and acceleration that it sparked something deep inside her, something burning of its own accord, the heat of desire she'd felt imagining the fire-heart of the forest entering her body. She ran to them.

The first human happened upon the second, third, and fourth, tangled in a writhing ball of desire, there at the origin. The fourth human had her mouth over the mouth of the third human, then the second, breathing in what they exhaled, exhaling again something new, for someone new, *for him!* thought the first human, rushing to the others and kneeling to drink in the kiss the fourth human had for him. Hot, hot breath came out and so did the smell of a burning forest, a sweet and acrid stink-scent the first human could taste in his mouth, play with on his tongue, and swallow even, though it was his duty to pass it on, this thing they breathed. The humans had their hands everywhere, they were wet, and hot; they were on fire and putting each other out; they were so vigorous in their devotion to the search for breath that they wore a smooth crater in the soft earth where they lay. They kissed, and stroked, and rubbed, and the friction and the heat kept them going. They were an engine; they burned clean though. They were dirty, sinking into the earth itself, sending up geysers of dust. In the end, it wasn't earth, or fire, or water, or even air that they were meant to breathe; it was the sylphs of love, from man-mother to man-father and back again, that kept these children of the Creator-Spirit burning hot as the Earth herself swallowed them up.

UNREFLECTED

BY PETER TIERYAS LIU ────────────

An autopsy of time would expose midnight at this LA rave as a buildup of greedy seconds poisoned by impatience. I've often wondered what it'd be like to split my brain open, unravel my memories like noodles that'd squirm because I'd boiled them too long. Melancholy weaves her way around my noodle and I split into a million different versions of myself.

I'm attending the event because an old colleague is catering and I'm assisting. The theme is Locust, or hunger, a charitable masquerade pretending to empathize with the impoverished and destitute. There's thousands who've starved the whole week to gather at this factory on the outskirts of town and smoke exotic herbs to alter their perceptions. Many of the women resemble spirits with all the smoke around us, rippling into thin mirages that meander frenetically. What would a lifetime with any of them be like? I spot a Chinese girl who's statuesque enough to fit into Roman porn with her chipped breasts and ivory ass. She notices my glance, approaches, and introduces herself as "Ella. I combined the Spanish words for the feminine and masculine 'the.'"

"I'm Byron," I reply.

She shakes my hand. "Tell me a secret."

"Why don't you go first?" I suggest.

She simpers. "I've lost my reflection."

"What do you mean?"

"Let me show you."

She pulls me into the girl's bathroom and points at the mirror. I see my ugly self and twenty girls behind, but no Ella.

"I thought I was dead at first," she says. "I still had to eat and shit so I figured I was alive." I stare to make sure she's real. She is, and I'm hypnotized by her skimpy dress and lean legs that are longer than my whole body. For a second, I wonder what it'd be like to bite them—frail, fragile, like a gaunt strip of quail. She asks me, "Do you think I'm beautiful?"

"How long's it been since you've seen yourself?"

"A year?" she shrugs. "I don't remember how I look anymore." Her skin is pale and the veins in her neck are vulnerably bulbous, throbbing with platelets and plasma. The excess plasma makes her ponder, "Do you have parts of yourself you hate seeing? I remember when I was a kid, a swarm of bees stung my arm till it was a bloody strip of bumps."

"I kill bees whenever I can," I reply.

"Why?"

"Cause the taste of honey makes me sick."

She asks me eight more questions, but she doesn't really care for an answer, more in love with her questions than her token boy of the moment. We spit through vodka shots. She wants to dance, tells me she's picked me as her date for the night. "Impress me," she says. "Or make me weep."

The confused expression on my face makes her laugh and she confesses she used to be a runway model traveling the globe, shuffling through French, Turkish, and Japanese lovers. "I dated a guy with the biggest knife collection in the world." She twirls her wrist in a slashing motion. "I made sure he was miserable while I was with him."

"Why?"

"I do it to every guy I love. It's their punishment since I know it can't last. What's your passion?"

"I used to be a chef," I answer.

"But?"

"But I quit after I lost my sense of taste and smell."

"You don't smell anything?"

I shake my head. "It was the dumbest mistake of my life. I had to try every exotic food, ate something in India that nearly killed me."

She puts something next to my nose. It crawls up my nostril like a scared roach.

"There's no such thing as a mistake. Only discontent after the fact," she says.

"I was too greedy," I reply, feeling dizzy.

She slaps me in the face, takes me to the bathroom. The mirror rises up like a barricade. Neither of us are reflected. I turn to her, shocked. She laughs and asks, "It doesn't matter what you've done if you can't see your reflection."

"But I want to see."

"Then shatter the glass with your fist."

When I hesitate, she smiles. "You never told me a secret."

Before I can answer, she turns around. A second later, she's vanished. I can't see her anywhere.

THE DRAGON'S GATE

BY SHANNON WENDT

Zachariah Avery grimaced as the tattooist pushed colorful ink into his skin. The high-pitched whine of the tattoo machine was grating on his nerves. The sensation on his arm varied from a warm but pleasant massage to sharp, grinding pain, as if his bone were being chipped away by a miniature jackhammer. Most of the time, it was just painfully annoying. He stared straight ahead, trying to let his mind go blank, while remaining perfectly still in the awkward position the tattooist had placed him in. He focused on a spot in the wall's texture that resembled a sea turtle. Inhale. Exhale. Inhale. Exhale.

Four months ago, a long-haul driver had fallen asleep at the wheel, and his forty-ton rig had mowed down his parents' sedan. It had taken the fire department ten hours to cut their bodies from the wreckage.

Zach was alone now. At twenty-two, he had no family to speak of, no close friends, no work associates. It wasn't until his parents' death that he realized he had been alive but not truly living all this time. He had lived with his parents for the whole of his life; he even attended a local college so he could keep living at home. His had been a shared existence, a half-life.

Now, he found himself a semi-grown-up who didn't know how to make decisions, friends, or dinner. It was time to evolve into a fully-fledged person, and this tattoo symbolized his first, tentative step into the waters of independent life. As he stared at the wall, he imagined the potential—the could-be, would-be, will-be—of his future.

The buzzing stopped. The tattooist wiped down Zach's arm with alcohol. The burning sensation instantly ceased. The skin felt cool, fresh, and vibrant. Like a phoenix rising from the ashes, it had been reborn. For Zach, this was the culmination of a personal quest. With this tattoo, he felt he was starting his life anew, a fresh, almost spiritual re-beginning.

The reflection in the mirror was breathtaking. It looked as if a Japanese watercolor master had used his arm as a canvas on which to create his life's masterpiece. The white-and-gold koi fish looked magnificent. The king of his lair. His scales seemed to shimmer, his gills seemed just on the brink of breathing. He strongly swam upstream in azure waters the color of the sky on a cloudless midsummer's afternoon. The water parted to make way for him in graceful arcing waves. Cherry blossoms fell as if to grace his presence with a ticker-tape parade of pink and white. It was glorious!

Zach tried to convey all this to the tattooist who had created it from ink and flesh with steel. "Wow, it's great," was all he could manage. He had never been any good at communicating with people. His brain simply froze when he had to talk to strangers.

Within a day, the tattoo had clouded over, as the tattooist had said it would. Looking at it now was like trying to appreciate a fine painting through milk-glass goggles. Zach was impatient to see it again in all its glory, but until then he kept up the ritual of cleansing it and feeding it creams and lotions several times a day.

Over the next week, it began to molt, just as real koi fish do after an illness or serious injury. Although it itched something fierce, Zach let the flaking skin be and just patted it with lotion—which he thought of as food for his tattooed fish—from time to time.

Finally on the eighth night, while Zach was asleep, the koi fish re-emerged from its healing process, spectacular and mighty. Zach fancied he could feel it breathing there in his arm. During a particularly vivid dream, he imagined it had risen up and launched itself free of his skin to taste the dark night air.

When he woke up, the koi was embedded in the translucent canvas of his skin in all of its Technicolor radiance. As he showered that morning, Zach imagined he could feel the fish rejoicing, splashing to and fro in the stream of falling water, drinking up its fresh bounty. After toweling off, he fed the tattoo some cream, and the ink seemed to absorb it and grow even more vibrant than before.

Every man (and some of the women) who frequented The Daily Grind Coffee Shop was enamored of Isabel de la Paz, one of the baristas who worked there. They couldn't help be entranced by her classical beauty—strong nose, delicate cheekbones, wavy black hair, and full lips, which were always slightly open as if offering a kiss. Born in Spain, she spoke perfect English, albeit with a slightly exotic, sibilant accent.

Zach ordered his usual breakfast—a large, black, house-roast coffee and a cheese Danish. As Isabel handed him his coffee, Zach's tattoo suddenly became warm and tingly—as if he'd been leaning his arm against a radiator. The sensation startled him, and his arm jerked as he took the coffee cup from Isabel. Hot coffee cascaded over the counter and the cup fell to the ground, empty and steaming. Zach found himself holding Isabel's hand, although he didn't remember taking it.

He released her hand. "Sorry about that." He smiled into her warm, brown eyes. "Would you like to have dinner with me sometime?"

She tilted her head as if considering his offer, surely not the first she had received that day. "I would love to have dinner with you. Tonight?"

Zach didn't know what had come over him today, but he was elated. He floated on his own personal cloud of confidence. As he went about his job as a bike messenger, he spoke to people when he'd never so much as made eye contact before. He joked with his boss, got to know some of the other messengers, and practically strutted as he made deliveries to uptight lawyers in posh office buildings.

His date with Isabel went swimmingly. They were still engaged in animated conversation two hours after the waiter had removed their dessert plate—a shared tiramisu. He walked her to her duplex, kissed her tenderly on the dimple of her chin and then her full, open lips, before wishing her a good night.

That night, he dreamed of swimming naked with a giant, gold-and-white koi fish in cool, invigorating waters.

Four months later, Zach was sharing a picnic with Isabel in a local park. They lay lazily on the verdant, velvety grass, holding hands. His tattoo had felt warm all day and was getting noticeably hotter.

Over the months since his tattoo had awakened from its healing slumber, Zach had learned to feel what he thought of as his koi fish's mood. Cold meant "Beware. Danger. Back off." Warm and tingly meant "Act now. Take charge." He hadn't told anyone about his "magic," confidence-inspiring tattoo, and he never would. After all, who would believe him? He hardly did himself. But this new intuition hadn't failed him yet.

He reached into the pack on the back of his bicycle and pulled out a small, red, leather box.

"Isabel de la Paz, will you spend the rest of your life with me?"

• • •

Zach had asked Isabel where she wanted to honeymoon, but she said she would rather put the money they would have spent on a fancy wedding and honeymoon into fixing up their home—the house Zach had lived in all his twenty-three years and had inherited from his parents.

He couldn't say "no" to his Isabel, and at least in this, she was being practical. So, they opted for a simple civil ceremony, and Zach put $75,000 of his inheritance toward remodeling their old Victorian house to Isabel's liking.

He had hoped that they would make some of the decisions together, but Isabel made each and every one unilaterally. Zach didn't mind too much—after all, she should feel at home.

They would of course be sharing the master bedroom, which he still thought of as his parent's room, a sacrosanct space. But it wouldn't make sense for them to sleep in his old bedroom instead. It was time for him to grasp the reins of adulthood and take up the mantle of the master bedroom.

One evening after work, he came home to find the master bedroom redone. It was painted a light, warm gray (a "new neutral" according to the designer Isabel had hired) and had linens and curtains in various shades of white. It looked fresh, but also cold and clinical. It wasn't as warm and inviting as his parent's old bedroom.

Then he noticed the mantel over the fireplace. The collection of framed photos of his parents had been replaced with impersonal objects d'art, faux flowers, and some pottery.

"Oh, I put them in storage," Isabel explained.

"But they're pictures of my parents!"

"I never met them. You said I should make it so I feel at home. I won't have strangers watching me sleep."

His tattoo was silent on the matter, so he compromised. "I'll put the photos in the game room, then."

That night, sleeping in the unfamiliar space that used to be his parents' bedroom, Zach dreamed of a fish out water, gills flapping desperately, drowning in air.

● ● ●

"Zach, you're twenty-five years old. Don't you think it's time to get a real job? You have a degree. You should do something with it."

Zach licked white frosting off his finger. Why did they have to do this today of all days?

"But I like being a messenger. The pay is decent, plus I still have a lot of my inheritance. And my free time is my own. I can spend more time with you, with our kids . . . "

"Zach, how can we even think about starting a family if you won't grow up?"

Isabel's brown eyes were flat and cold, her lips drawn tight and tense. She wasn't pretty when she scowled like this, which was more and more often.

Zach sighed. "I promise to look for a new job tomorrow. But can we please just enjoy my birthday today?"

● ● ●

Dylan was turning five today, and Zach was going to miss it. It was quarterly review and everyone at the firm was working overtime, especially the managers.

He had let Sally, one of the hardest workers under him, go home at six o'clock so she could attend her daughter's dance recital. Now, Zach and the rest of his team would have to take up the slack. He hoped he'd be home before midnight.

He'd promised to call Isabel to let her know when he might make it home.

"Hi, Isabel. It's going to be a late one. We're short-staffed, and we have to make tomorrow's deadline or there'll be hell to pay."

"OK, we'll manage without you."

"Love you, 'Bel. And give the birthday boy a kiss from me."

Click.

She never said "I love you" or even "bye" any more. He felt his heart contract.

He made it home at one-thirty A.M., exhausted and thinking of his freckled, blond, five-year-old boy.

Isabel was still up, sitting at the dining room table, doing nothing. She was in one her moods again. He kissed her cheek. She jerked her head away, said nothing.

"I'm going to go up and give Dylan his present."

"No, don't wake him. It's a school night. You always get him too excited."

"That's because we rarely get to see each other. Come on, 'Bel. It's as much for me as it is for him."

"No. It's not important. It can wait until morning."

His koi fish tattoo had been silent for the past six years. He was beginning to think he had imagined it ever turning hot or cold. Still, before any confrontation or major decision, he was in the habit of feeling or "listening" to see if his tattoo had anything to say on the matter. Nothing. It was just a regular arm with ordinary ink.

"I'll just go up and peek in on him, then. I promise not to wake him."

Dylan was sleeping on his side, his cheek flattened, hair ruffled, mouth slightly open. He was wearing the striped pajamas that he said was what young wizards like himself wore to bed. Clutched in his hand was a plastic wand, a birthday gift from one of his friends. Zach imagined that Dylan was having happy, young wizard dreams filled with magic birthday cakes and enchanted parties. He remembered when his life was so simple and filled with wonder, sparked by imagination. It seemed so long ago.

Dylan woke up, smiled, and waved at his dad. Zach put his finger up to his mouth, making the international "shhhh" gesture. He mouthed "Happee birth-day!" Dylan grinned and waved his magic wand. "Ver-ry nice! See you in the morn-ning." He blew Dylan a kiss, closed the door with a quiet click, and went to bed.

As long as his day had been, Zach was having difficulty falling asleep. His mind was troubled. He had been aware for a long time that he was profoundly unhappy with his life. Work was a soul-draining experience—he no longer felt fulfilled by a job well done, by promotions or accolades, or even his paycheck and 401(k). His marriage to Isabel had been a mistake from the start. He had been in denial at first, but now he couldn't refute that it just didn't work for either of them. She was cold where he was warm. Dylan was his sole joy.

If he turned away from Isabel, what repercussions would that have in Dylan's life? Would he become a little-boy-lost like so many children of divorce? Would the damage be worse if he stuck it out with Isabel and made-believe that they were a happy couple?

Zach knew what he would do if Dylan hadn't existed. But Dylan had been born. And what was best for Dylan mattered most of all.

When Zach eventually dozed off, he dreamed of going fishing. He cast his rod in a long, floating arc. The pond rippled in overlapping, concentric circles. A giant, gold-and-white koi fish surfaced, un-snared. The fish stared straight at him and its mouth moved, but he couldn't understand what it was saying. He didn't speak fish anymore but remembered that he once had.

Zach and Dylan walked through the park, enjoying a rare Saturday afternoon together.

"Dylan, we need to have a serious talk, man to young wizard."

"OK, Daddy."

"You know that your mom and I both love you, right?"

Dylan nodded.

"Well, if your mom and I no longer live together, we'll still love you just as much. Do you understand?"

Another nod, but now Dylan looked worried. "Daddy, who would I live with? You or Mommy?"

"Well, that depends. Most likely, you'd live with your mom some of the time and with me some of the time."

Dylan pondered this for a few minutes, twirling his plastic wand. "When I'm with you, will you work all the time like now?"

For the briefest flicker, Zach thought he felt his tattoo flare warm, but it passed so quickly he decided it must've been just a muscle twitch.

He squatted down until he was eye-level with his son, and put his hands gently on Dylan's head, stroking his hair. "Dylan, I promise that when it's our time together, you'll have my undivided attention. It will be so much better than now. Cross my heart, little man."

"Daddy, I'm a wizard!"

"Right. Of course. I stand corrected, young wizard." He tickled his son until he squirmed with glee.

On Monday morning, Zach woke up, alone in bed (as usual), a good fifteen minutes before the alarm went off. His to-do list rotated through his thoughts: 1) Quit his job. 2) Break up with Isabel. 3) Contact a lawyer (ugh). 4) Celebrate with Dylan.

He didn't remember the last time he'd been so happy, so excited. He started a pot of coffee brewing and made his morning ablutions in record time.

He poked his head into the guest bedroom where Isabel now slept and told her she could sleep in, that he would take Dylan to school.

"It's time for all young wizards to rise and shine! Come on, Dylan, wakey-wakey."

As they both ate a hearty breakfast of Loopy-Loops cereal that turned the milk a lavender hue, they discussed the intricacies of a young wizard's schooling. Dylan didn't think that letters and numbers were important for wizards, that they were better off learning to draw or make wands—something more useful.

"Books are magical, Dylan. Just wait until you learn to read. You'll see. In fact, why don't I start teaching you? There's no reason you have to wait until first grade."

While Dylan sat at the dining table, drawing in his coloring book filled with black-and-white images of young wizards at play, Zach got dressed for work. He first put on his suit and tie, then took it all off, leaving it on the ground in a wrinkling heap. "Screw that," he mumbled, and put on a T-shirt and shorts instead.

"You can't quit without giving at least two weeks' notice!" His boss, Frank, who had as much personality as his name indicated, was becoming dangerously rubicund, flushing from temple to too-tight necktie knot. Zach hoped he had taken his blood pressure medicine.

"I think you'll find I can." Zach's calm air contrasted with Frank's apoplexy.

"You'll get no recommendation if you quit on me like this, you . . . you . . . quitter!" Frank's spittle was flying now.

"I don't need a recommendation. There's nothing you can do to stop me from quitting without notice."

Now that he was free from this meaningless, soul-siphoning job, he looked at Frank with empathy instead of animosity.

"I wish you the best, Frank. Really I do. But I have to do what's right for me. And this is it. Goodbye, Frank."

Everyone stared at Zach as he made his way from the fourth floor where Frank had a corner office, down the elevator, through the lobby. Not only was his attire inappropriate enough to garner stares, but Zach couldn't stop smiling. His grin was over-large, ridiculous, and frankly starting to hurt his cheeks, but there it was. He couldn't get rid of it. People acted as if he'd been transmogrified into a clown or The Joker—an aberration of correct corporate culture.

"What's gotten into him?" they whispered as he passed by.

"I don't know, but he'll never make it if he pulls any more stunts like this."

If Isabel was surprised that Zach was home at 11 A.M., she didn't show it. She didn't say hello, or ask why he was home early, or whether he wanted to get an early lunch out—a special treat. She merely glanced at him once and went back to reading the paper.

"'Bel, we need to talk." He took a gulp of air and decided to just get right to the point. "I want a divorce."

She looked up from her newspaper briefly. "OK," she said. Then she went back to reading. She read for several minutes, turning the pages and everything, as if she found the local news more engrossing than her family's moment of crisis.

"'Bel, I want to keep the house." He paused, thought for a second, and blurted, "And full custody of Dylan."

"That's fine. I want a quarter-of-a-million dollars."

And that was that. It was both more painless than he expected and more painful. He wasn't grinning like The Joker now. He felt as if he were suffocating, but he knew as the weeks and months passed, he would recover. And he would have Dylan by his side while he did.

Isabel stayed at the table until she had finished reading the paper, folded it, and put it down.

"I'll just get some of my things. In case you need me, I'll be staying with Steve Ericson."

Dr. Steve Ericson was Dylan's pediatrician. As it turned out, Isabel and Dr. Steve were very close friends and had been for years.

• • •

"Daddy, Daddy, Daddy! There's a fish in the bathtub! A magic fish!" Dylan bounced on the bed.

Zach tried to clear the grogginess from his head. He checked the alarm clock. 6:36 A.M. A bit early for magic fish, but he was happy to see Dylan so excited. He had been a bit glum since his mother left.

"'Morning, Dylan. Did I hear something about a magic fish?"

"Yes! Come see!" Dylan jumped out of bed and grabbed his dad by the hand, pulling him like an exuberant little tug boat.

Zach realized he needed to pee something fierce, but it could wait until he checked the bathtub.

The tub was filled to the rim; water cascaded over the side as the fish— a real fish—swam carefully in the too-small tub. It was the largest koi fish Zach had ever seen. It had shimmering gold and white scales. It gave Zach a look—a knowing look.

He recognized this fish. It was his fish. His tattooed fish.

He looked down at his arm. The tattoo was gone. He checked the mirror. Not a trace of it remained. Not a scale or whisker or wave or cherry blossom. His arm was skin-toned, freckled, and completely unfamiliar to him.

"Daddy! What's that on your back?"

Zach craned his neck around to get a look in the mirror. His entire back was covered with a brand new tattoo.

What he saw in the mirror was astonishing. A golden dragon had taken residence in the musculature of his back. It was so large that it meandered in an S-shape from his scapula to his coccyx. Its scales were so detailed, so perfect, they looked real, like he himself had grown scales. He touched his back, but it was smooth skin. The dragon had animated, blue eyes. It seemed to be grinning and sticking out its forked tongue as if in jest.

"Daddy, it's a dragon!" Dylan said in awe. "Can I touch it?"

As father and son worked at digging the large pit that would be the koi pond, Zach told Dylan the legend of the fish that becomes a dragon for the third time that day.

"Once, there was a little koi fish. He had always lived in a pond with his parent fishes. It was the only life he knew . . . "

As the years passed, Dylan grew up and outgrew wizarding, but still he learned to speak fish.

Zach still communed with the giant gold-and-white koi fish they called "Dragon." Sometimes he spoke aloud, but sometimes he just sat on a stone bench by the koi pond and thought his thoughts. At the end of their "conversations," Zach always felt more clear-headed, more sure of himself and his decisions.

He imagined that Dragon would live for generations more, and that Dylan's kids and grandkids would learn to "speak fish" as he and Dylan did. He also got Dragon some regular koi fish for piscine companionship. Perhaps they would mate, and their children would be extraordinary, too.

WORD PAINTING OF A PSYCHIATRIST

BY CAROLINE HAGOOD

When I first saw you,
curled in the toadstool of my mind's eye,
I wanted to learn how to paint
so that I could explain colorly
the conversation of your skin tones,
the shock talk of hues that was your body.

I wanted to convey the pickled awe
at the inside of my throat as I looked on you.
Even at sixteen, I knew what you were: wunderkammer,
a madness of sense-awakening things,
astonishment soup and wonder mushrooms
in a boy shape, you most treasured
cabinet of curiosities, you.

But I cannot paint, so I explain you wordily.
First, I talk about your very dark hair,
much-coveted and positively full of wolves.
It moves when you move, as though you were
the wind blowing that hairy planet.
Blackstar, blackbird, fly me somewhere
on those unfathomable strands.

Next I talk about your smile.
Wry on the rocks, Cheshire-Cat-style,
a jaunty, crooked marvel, peeking out of
conspicuously unsmiling crowds, like a frozen margarita

in a world of compulsory milk,
that moves when you talk, but never leaves.

Then I describe your ears, a little big, maybe,
but this is what makes them perfect.
One day, I have a wild vision of swimming in them,
an ear-fish in waxy waters. While inside,
I discover that those aural cavities of yours are awash
with Thumbelinas and convenience stores for fairy folk.
As I leave, I swear I see the tiny headlights of a clown troupe
spreading out of your acoustic organs, lighting my way.

Finally, I add your eyes to the equation.
Neck plus shoulders plus these shining things equals you:
Someone who crouches close to see the villagers' pain,
peers into brain valves and mind machinery,
eases the ache of neural connections,
goes at endless melancholy with a wrench.
I remember when I was crying and you
told me with those nervy orbs everything I needed.
I knew then that this is what you did for all those people
in your factory of gentleness,
where you keep the invisible things
that matter most to people.

ODE TO JACK SKELLINGTON

BY JADE MILLER

Jack, I think you're quite a swell guy.
It doesn't matter you're all bones
and don't have beautiful blue eyes.
I can gaze deeply into those hollow sockets
and lose myself as you tuck our clasped hands
into your classy suit pocket.

Why, oh why
would you choose Sally over I?
I may not be made of fabric, and have hair of yarn,
but I more than make up for it with my charm.
My skin will feel like fire under your fingertips,
give some feeling of life back into your lips.

The Pumpkin King and I were meant to be,
Jack, don't you see?
I'll care for Zero as if he were my own
and make us a nice, cozy little home.
If I must, I'll join you under the ground
to live out the rest of our lives in Halloween Town.

THE MERMAID'S GIFT

BY MICHAEL C. KEITH

Do you know the reward for combing a mermaid's hair?"

The fisher-boy shakes his head, his sea-colored eyes as unreadable as the moon.

I lean forward, slapping my tail in the surf. The water sprays up around us, cool and salty-sweet. My newly combed hair feels like a cloud flowing around my shoulders. "Three wishes. Anything you can think of, I can grant you."

"But at what cost?"

I laugh. A flock of seagulls circles, answering the sound with their own low cries. "I see you've heard the stories—and been wise enough to listen. That is rare in one so young." With one webbed hand, I trace the smooth line of his cheekbones. "And one so fair. But if you know the stories, surely you can outwit me."

He flinches out of my grasp. "I know I cannot."

"Ah. You are wise indeed, young master." I touch his face again, just with my fingertips, and this time, he does not pull away. "But will you be foolish enough not to accept my gift?"

"I have nothing to wish for."

"No?" I lift a fistful of sand from the beach between us and let the grains run out between my fingers. When I open my hand again, three tiny shells sit in my palm. "Then take these . . . When you need me, whisper your wish into the shell, and I will grant it."

"Thank you." He takes the shells warily, tucking them into his pocket and taking up his net.

By the time he wades back into the sea, I am already gone.

● ● ●

"I wish my wife could get with child."

I do not recognize the voice at first; it has been years since our chance encounter on the beach. But as I surface and breathe in the cool night air, I remember the eyes.

The boy—a man now—looks startled to find himself standing on the beach.

"Oh," he says, and kneels down beside me. "Did you hear my wish?"

"Yes." I take his rough, work-hardened hands in mine. They are still warm from the sun. "You wished for a child."

"Can you grant it?"

"Of course."

"Good." He pulls his hands away.

As he turns and walks back to the village, I open my fingers and see what he has left there. A tiny conch glistens wetly in the moonlight.

● ● ●

"I wish my wife could give birth."

This time, he does not look surprised. As I emerge from the sea, he tosses a shell at me and steps back, out of my reach.

"She's bleeding—the doctor's say uncontrollably." His voice is flat, but I see his fists clenching at his sides. "I want her healthy, and I want the child to live. Can you grant it?"

"Of course." His pain makes him beautiful. I nearly ache with longing, but I do not try to touch him.

"Good," he says, and walks back up the beach toward the village.

● ● ●

"I wish my daughter was healthy."

He starts to hand the shell to me; but this time, I pull away.

"This is your last wish, you know."

His eyes glisten but do not move.

"Are you sure this is what you want?"

"My daughter is dying. How could I want anything else?"

I shrug, brushing hair away from my face. "You could let her die and wish for your wife's next child to be perfect. Haven't you heard the stories?"

"I have, but that is not what I want."

"You could wish to live forever. You would have an eternity to make a perfect daughter."

"That is not what I want." He drops the shell into the sand. "I wished for my child to be healthy. Can you grant it?"

"Of course," I sigh.

"Then do it."

• • •

The seagulls hear him coming before I do. They call to me with their laughing voices, beckoning me to shore.

When I surface, I find him sitting on the beach, his face buried in his hands.

"I want my child healed," he whispers.

"I already healed her. It was your last wish, remember?"

He shakes his head. "She's sick again. There's nothing the doctors can do. Please, heal her again."

"I'm sorry, but I cannot. It was your last wish."

He reaches for me. I let him touch my face, run his fingers through my hair. "Please. I'll do anything."

"It only works once."

"I know; I've heard the stories. Now we talk of cost." He leans forward, until our foreheads touch, and his sea-eyes fill my vision. "If I offered to trade my life for my child's, could you do it?"

"No," I say. My heart pounds in my chest like a wild thing against the bars of its cage. "I won't do it. Do you know what happens when a mermaid accepts aid from a mortal?"

"I've heard the stories. I know you've fallen in love."

I press my lips against his. He doesn't pull away—but neither does he return my kiss. "Then how can you ask me for such a thing?" I whisper. "How can you ask me to take your life?"

"If you truly understood love, you would know how."

I sob, plead, but he won't listen. He gently pushes me away and stands, turning towards the village.

"Where are you going?"

"To find someone who can help me."

"No, please!" I swallow salt and bitterness. "Don't leave me. I'll do it."

For the first time, I see a smile spread across his face.

He kneels again and offers his hands to me, but I don't take them.

I lift a tiny shell from the beach and grind it to powder in my hand. The magic rises in my chest, fierce and strong as the tides. I spread my arms like wings and fling myself into the ocean.

Through the darkness, I see his daughter. As water fills my lungs, I see color return to her corpse-pale face. As cold bites into my bones, I see her sit up in bed, stand, walk across the room.

As sea-foam envelops me, I see her father take her into his arms.

TWO-THIRDS A LOVE POEM

BY NICK CHANDLER

I f I could just touch your
ankle
like a light and hollowed
breeze
whose breath tugs at your
hemline,
then, in a slip, recedes
back into
the new world, over old
and fresh-built
homes as it remembers
itself, cold and ephemeral,
hungry and lost, as it
grazes more feet
and laps at the misty
heated windows.

DANCING IN THE AIR

BY SHWETA NARAYAN

The Raja's youngest hostage dances high above the ground along the stately walls of Junagarh Fort. From window lattice to red-stone column, he leaps, now curling, rolling, bounding off a ledge; now hanging one-handed and still. No prison can hold him, the swordsmaster's son, except the ring of gold about his neck. Light and shadow play across the collar's graven spells and symbols. Flecks of sweat fly from the boy, glinting like diamonds in the sunlight. A drop, a catch, a serpent's arch; he flips into an alcove and dances around the red-stone elephant god.

The swordsmaster does not look up. He teaches the guardsmen—his captors, his foes—to strike in perfect time. Their dusty white courtyard gleams with steel and pride. The swordsmaster is banded with heavy gold, etched and scratched into dullness. And he is bandaged, his left hand missing one finger.

The guardsmen do not look up at the small and sun-reddened boy. They know his golden collar will bring him to ground, in time, as it did his father. But his father is the swordsmaster, and though the swordsmaster is now but a man, he is yet a man of sharp and shining blades. Deep in the alcove, seen only by the elephant god, the dancing boy takes from his belt his father's final gift: a single claw of rainbowed, chiseled diamond. And he slices the collar from his neck. When two half circles of sunlight fall tumbling to the ground, the swordsmaster looks up at last, smiles, and cuts down one guard, then another, teaching them how little he has taught them. He smiles still as they rally, as they fence him in with steel, laughs at the terror behind that steel, and glances up for one last sight: looping, liquid crimson coiling sinuous from the alcove; the flash of scales on spreading wings against the searing sky.

HOUSE OF GLASS

BY RUTH DOMINGUEZ

I live in a glass house
of rumors
violent whispers
from fiery tongues

in the winter the ice perpetually
creeps forward, inching slowly
and retreating again from the
heat
like the oceans' tide

during the night
frost decorates
the windows in icy formations
of various fractions and angles

and during sunrise
they melt away
peel away
the clear view of
snow

the sun is my friend and enemy
in my glass house i accept sun rays
in their full force
on cloudless days

sunset is nostalgic
and dusk is the
haunting
lonesome love
of dying lovers

i observe the sun's
ever-changing
color of the world
from views in my glass house

my pipes are glass
and even my waste
is delicately seeped in solar energy
i flush, shower,
and gargle in the sun

in the evening i climb
my winding-stair of glass
comb my hair with a glass comb
lay flat on my bed
and wait for the sky
to deepen
and be pierced with star-light

my motion on the orbiting,
rotating earth,
is as a jagged clear crystal
a fossil

with life-breath

victim of fog
and storm

sun's companion

THE QUAIL'S HEART

BY CHRISTINE STODDARD

In a land neither here nor there, roamed a stressed—some might say aggrieved—quail. If she had had thumbs, she would have twiddled them until they became raw. Instead, she had wings, and she dared not twiddle those because she feared her feathers would fall out. That would not do for such a vain little creature. Thus, she continued agonizing over the plight of motherhood with all of her feathers intact.

If the quail could have hired a surrogate mother, she would've made the phone call right away. But such an option does not yet exist for quails. And even if it did, they would have to begin using phones and printing their own phone book first. Otherwise, how would anyone get in touch with a surrogate?

The quail hated motherhood for several reasons. She did not look forward to her plump figure becoming even plumper. She also decided that, with a lifespan of only four or five years, it did not seem just that she should have to spend at least half of it tending to hungry, shrieking "goblins." The quail did not want to find seed for anyone but herself. She figured she exercised enough as it was.

After bitterly carrying eighteen little eggs inside of herself for months, the quail laid them as quickly as could. With her lady parts still sore, she promptly left the eggs to attend a retreat. Being a quail, she had no nails and therefore did not consider getting a "mani" or "pedi," though, being as vain as she was, the quail would've if she could've. But sitting and complaining about motherhood to other animal mothers instead of to a nail technician seemed fine to her.

The retreat was called "Motherhood Circle." It took place atop the highest mountain in the area. Feeling too tired and lazy to make the trek herself, the quail hopped onto the hind-leg of an unassuming doe who happened to be heading in the same direction. At just the right point, the doe bent down to munch the sweet grass that only grew on that mountain. The quail tumbled off of the deer's leg, straightened out her feathers, and strutted over to the Motherhood Circle.

A chubby gopher guru overlooked a small gathering of retreat-goers from his fungus throne. His bright eyes and calmly still ears gave him the look of someone fully at peace. The quail appreciated his air of wisdom. It made her feel like she was getting her money's worth.

The gopher guru led all the new mothers—a horse, a fox, a raccoon, and, of course, the quail—through a few breathing exercises to start. They stood, closed their eyes, and risked appearing a tad ridiculous. The quail worried that a handsome male quail might see her. Consequently, she refused to shut her eyes or "roar like a lioness."

After they had all practiced breathing, the animals plopped down on beds of moss. Except for the gopher guru, of course. He gracefully sat down on his fungus throne.

"Now," said the gopher guru, "you should all feel more relaxed."

The animals nodded.

"Let us introduce ourselves." He paused and smiled brilliantly. "Please state your name, loudly and clearly and tell us how many children you have and how long you've been a mother."

The horse went first. "My name is Willow Blossom, I have one foal, and I've been a mother for eight months. My daughter's nearly a yearling already! I'm so proud of how smart and beautiful she's grown up to be."

The other animals put their paws and wings together in applause.

Then the fox spoke. "My name is Lily Pad, I have two kits, and I've been a happy mother for five full months. I'm so sad that I've reached the half-way mark already."

The crowd, barring the quail, issued a collective "Aw!" Again, the animals clapped.

The raccoon followed. "I'm River Reed and I've been a mother of three for almost a year, like Willow Blossom. I'm not ready to let them go! I love them so much." The raccoon grabbed a leaf from the forest floor to dry her eyes.

After the animals clapped, they turned to the quail, who had not been quick to share.

"How long have you been a mother?" the gopher guru prompted.

The quail paused before shouting in a manic frenzy. "One day! Just one day! I laid the eggs this morning and then I ran away! I couldn't deal with motherhood!" She wept as melodramatically as she could manage.

The other animals stared at the quail, their jaws slung open.

"Alright," the gopher guru said as he straightened his posture and stood up from his fungus throne, "You girls know what to do."

The gopher whipped out a knife and lunged toward the quail. The other animals did not hesitate to take his lead. In an instant, the gopher had cut out the quail's heart, shaken it in the air, and then tore it into teeny chunks for the other animals to eat.

In a land neither here nor there, eighteen quail eggs hatched without a mother, and a protein-deficient doe gulped up a heartless quail body.

The end.

ENLIGHTENMENTS

BY BENJAMIN NARDOLILLI

He showed up to the salon,
claiming that he had the solution to it all.
We thought he was like Newton,
inspired by the apple's fall.

He wore no wig, nor a silken shirt;
he wore a robe, hanging like a skirt.

"I am the way, the only way,"
with pompous pride, he said.
"Praise my father in heaven,
when I rise up from the dead."

We laughed and asked
if he had the slightest proof.
He turned a glass of water into wine,
and showed us Satan on the roof.

We said nothing and drank our tea.
We said it could be explained, scientifically:

The drink had changed from
striking the atoms in a fashion,
that made their ether vibrate.
This was the secret behind his passion.

WOLF'S RAIN

BY JON-O GAZDECKI

L ost under the moon,
howling to the stars above.
A wolf I am, brave.

Her eyes, they glow red.
Bloomed under the lunar light.
Paradise . . . She'll lead.

COQUETTE CORPSE

BY JOSEPHINE STONE

I've got a disease growing at the base of my spine
and I've become too cowardly to say if it's yours or if it's mine.
Inebriated whispers lay dormant at your neck, ears, and hips.
You kiss them good-bye as they each fall from your lips.
I try to catch them in my hands before they hit the ground.
They trickle through my fingers just to lay unfound.
Our skin pales and sinks tight against our bones
as we carry on with this dance and each joint bends and moans.
To keep time we're stepping on footprints so delicately placed
with my arms around your neck, and yours around my waist.
Tonight our bodies will gracefully collide,
prematurely soaked in a sweet formaldehyde.

HELLBENT & CHAPSTICK

BY CHRISTOPHER SLOCE

Tins of lip balm impress ovals into the seat of my khakis. My lips look like streets after earthquakes, the way my tongue attacks them, and in my younger years they called me "Pitbull" because of that habit. But I no longer buy ChapStick. I can't stand the smell or look. It makes me break into sweats even when my wife or someone in one of my classes put on lipstick. I have to sigh and say, "It's a mirage, Conner. Hold onto yourself." When they do this, I turn around and bite my lips.

I've thought about sewing pockets in my coats. Secret ones to hold my balm like Kennedy's barbiturates.

My vision is failing now. I don't wear Clubmasters anymore. I wear horn rims and plaid and corduroys and grey flannels. I stand in front of the mirror some mornings, knowing that long ago I'd have called myself a faggot.

I totaled two cars in my youth: one a cherry red Cavalier I drove into the side of a mountain, high more off the frenzied death beat of the Sex Pistols "Pretty Vacant" than any chemicals, despite my Ritalin and stale beer bender the night before. I totaled another car with a golf club. I thought killing his car would drive his lust away from whatever girl I, too, lusted for. I was hell with golf clubs.

The car I loved most was a Japanese-something with a hull that looked like it had caught a venereal disease. I brought violence to the gas pedal, angry at its insistence on tempting me.

I don't know what made me like that. I grew up in a nice little house with an apple tree in my front yard. I played Little League baseball. My high school classmates didn't esteem me, but they didn't torture me either; I just kind of blended in unnoticed. I still remember the first violent act

I ever committed, but I elect not to speak on it; we all find our own first lovemaking fascinating. It was the same each time—the subject plain: a girl reeking of polyester who took me into the boiler room at school (there are marks on my back to prove it) or a snot-nosed kid who kicked my favorite Tonka truck into a creek. After each incident, I desired to stand atop the nearest building, proclaim myself God of the place, and smite my challenger. It was my way of proving I had made it into a club of fist fighters and fornicators, of tough, salacious bastards.

So I chased that feeling—that desire to stand high and scream who I was and why I should be known, to make myself a suzerain and sultan of nothing in particular. Allow me to point out that I was no sociopath. I hit men when reasonable; they knew it was coming, and I never hit a woman. It was stupid behavior, but it was logical. This was my third birth, my heart pumping the pure speed that Ritalin highs could never touch. Society didn't reject me. I simply left. There were things I wanted and people attaching clanging, taunting bells to them. I wanted to please myself and hurt no one, so on nights I was alone I could look in the mirror and say, "I did okay." I wanted a life without regrets. The regrets come now at the sound of Johnny Rotten's siren yell or revving engines. Or when I see a pair of Clubmasters or ChapStick.

I was big and lovable with an undercurrent of brutality. The understanding was this: I would clock anyone who stepped to or looked like they would. I took nothing from no one. And when I gave it to them, it was with two well-worn ChapStick tubes in each palm, never used. And in the winter, when I kept my lips wet with my tongue, I convinced myself someone was coming for me or attempting to give to me something they might just regret.

There were many girls I wanted, plenty I had, but only Heather Thacker matters. She was tan and blonde and claimed to have Native American roots. I was very interested in her. The week before it happened, we went to the fair, sharing funnel cakes with sugar dust trapped in the weaves and watching ducks at the farm exhibit walk up the little steps to slide down into the dirty pool. The cotton candy looked like an outgrowth of her lips. Some nights I'd dream I'd go to her house and men would be gathered all around, and I'd look up at the full moon and watch my hands splay, my nails curve, and my face get long. And out of my mouth would come a deafening howl as I threw a man into the woods, and then I would wake, aching up and down, my mouth dripping. We'd lie in bed together, and I'd tell her my dreams.

I went to her house one day. She left her door unlocked, and I walked inside. They kept their washing machine and dryer in the kitchen.

"Hey," she said, coming into the room, a look of surprise on her face. She wore bad jeans and a worse sweatshirt. Two sheets, crimson mingled with cream, lay draped over the hamper between us.

"Jesus!" I shouted. "What happened to those?" I knew her answer would be either ashamed or awkward with an excuse.

"Oh, you know. Nothing."

"Ah."

Her face went red. "Randall McCoury came over." My nostrils flared, I imagined my fingernails getting longer. "I see. And you're washing those sheets why?"

She looked down, grabbed detergent, and acted as she had never seen it before, reading the instructions carefully. "I can't talk about it."

I wanted to howl but instead I said, "I don't like this. I should leave." I drove away from her house, my hair looking a bit longer in the mirror. I drove around until I found a big house on a hill with boarded-up doors. I laid waste to every window with a golf club, hoping the sky would go mauve and then velvet purple and I could scream and eat the dead wood. I slept in my car with my clothes covering me. Mom knew I was wont to come and go. The next day I awoke, dressed, lusted for red meat. I went to Dice's on Main, a diner. I walked inside, seeing the old men in golf jackets and windbreakers. Behind the counter, a Pepsi sign that was missing the S hung like a crown for Old Man Dice, who stood beneath it, smiling. I like to believe he expected me.

"Hey, Conner!" he shouted. I sat down.

"I'll have three hamburgers and a chocolate milk." The second I said *milk*, Randall McCoury walked inside. I knew him, and nothing had changed about him since the day I met him: he still had his bucked teeth, which I heard he made up for with great endowment. He wore a Yankees hat low on his head and gauze around his wrists. He sat beside me.

"Hey Sloan."

"How are you, McCoury?"

"Rough. Where you been?"

"About. Burning up roads."

"Yeah, you getting any lately?"

"I'll tell you if you tell me."

"I been seeing some people."

"Look at you, you big bastard! Anybody I know?"

"Nah."

"You sure?"

"Yeah, I'd think so."

My chocolate milk sat on the table. I took a sip of it. "What do you think about Heather Thacker? Thought I'd get your opinion."

"Yeah, she's cool," he said. I fished my ChapStick out of my pockets. With a single quick movement, I slapped the back of my palm against the bill of his Yankees hat, knocking it to the floor. He narrowed his eyes at me and took a step back. Bloody bandages covered the top of his head.

"Funny, I went to see her earlier. Her sheets looked like a pig got stuck on them. And she mentioned you."

He shrugged. I put the ChapStick down and I tore the tape off of his head. "OW! FUCK!" He shouted. Tiny cuts covered his temples. He ran to the bathroom, so I followed him. He stood at the sink. He took the bandages off his wrists. Blood flowed freely and his mouth quivered, "God, kill me." These weren't cuts. These were holes.

I left it to God without paying, ChapSticks in my hands.

I don't understand entirely how I got here, but I felt deep in my gut a thirst for words to describe McCoury's wounds. I sicken myself when I look back, hellbent on another's blood when they possibly couldn't control a thing.

And nights when I navel gaze so long I get sick, I fall asleep and dream of Randall McCoury, holding a flaming sword and wearing a white cloak, knocking me into dead woods while I beg for God to kill me.

THE EIGHTH WIFE

BY MEGAN ARKENBERG

Don't open the door, he said, and I listened to him. Listened because, like everyone else in his life, I was afraid.

Well, I thought, leaning against the tower wall to ease the burden on my laundry-bearing shoulders, if there was one thing my husband could cure a body of, it was fear. Oh, he was terrible in that first week of marriage, crashing around the dining room like an angry bull, dragging me up these steps to the door at the top of the tower and shaking a promise from me that I would not, absolutely would not open it. And then there were the stories—all his pretty little aristocratic ladies before me, carried off by consumption and apoplexy and what-not. Yes, consumption—as if those bitches had ever spent a night in the cold in their lives.

So of course I was frightened. But even I, silly little laundry maid that I was, could see the value in a marriage to Count Bluebeard—and he was, contrary to what the stories may have told you, most phenomenally handsome. It wasn't so bad. The drafts in the castle were loud, but not nearly as cold as those that came in through the gaps in my father's thatched roof—and if the rats were bigger than the ones at home, well, at least they didn't bite.

My husband, too, was not as cruel as he first appeared. His face, with its fierce blue-black hair and cold gray eyes, hid a soft, gentle—even submissive—heart. I vividly remember bringing him a plate of apples on the morning after our wedding, feeding them to him with my own hands—the soft scratch of his tongue on my fingers when he licked away the juice.

And so the fear went—not away, exactly, but into the far back of my mind, locked up like that room at the top of the tower.

With a sigh, I pushed myself away from the wall and started back down the stairs. The bronze ring in my pocket jingled with each step. My husband was away on business of his own; I had the castle nearly to myself, and he had entrusted me with the keys as well. All the keys. And for the thousandth time, I wondered what was behind that door he had told me never to open.

"Oh, hell," I said to the stone. I was his wife—didn't I have the right to know his secrets? I ducked into the nearest chamber and dropped my armload of silk and brocade and cambric onto the bed. Let the servants clean the laundry for once, though I knew they wouldn't do it as well as I. It was time for me to behave like the lady I was.

I took the stairs two and three at a time. My silk shoes slipped on the damp stone; I kicked them off halfway up and ran barefoot the rest of the way.

The door at the top was nothing fancy, just a few wooden boards bound with iron and stamped with a heavy black lock. I took the ring from my pocket and tried each key in turn. The one that fit—a massive greenish thing with cruel angels' faces carved in the metal—felt strangely warm and slimy, as though it had been dipped in blood.

That was a bad thought. I shuddered, turned the key, and pushed the door open.

A smell greeted me, dark and sweet as wine. I stepped into the room—the wooden floor was soft and cold beneath my feet—and looked around. The walls were damp, greenish with mold, and the edges of the windows were beginning to crumble. A solitary spider sat in her web between two of the rotting ceiling beams.

There was nothing else there.

I stood in the middle of the room, dumb with bewilderment, my hands slack at my sides. In a little while—perhaps a minute later, perhaps more—I heard footsteps on the stairs.

I knew when he stood in the doorway; the color went out of the walls, and the spider stopped spinning in her web.

"My love," he said softly. I turned to face him with a violent flush of shame. One strong hand gripped the door post, as if it was all that kept him upright; in the other hand, he held my silk slippers.

"I'm sorry," I croaked. "I didn't mean . . . "

He crossed the room and knelt on the floor in front of me. I could see the tears like ocean fog in his eyes. "I have denied you nothing," he said. "Not rose gardens or ballrooms or rooms filled with music, or sunlit parlors or libraries full of books. Everything in the castle is yours—everything but this."

He held one shoe out, like a prince in a very different story. Numbly, I slipped my foot into it.

"I hoped you could trust me," he said. "I hoped you would believe your own heart over the stories . . . "

His voice snapped—from anger or pain, I didn't know. He slid the other shoe onto my foot and remained kneeling, his forehead pressing against my stomach.

"This was all I had to call my own," he said. "Now it is yours."

"Wait," I said—foolishly, for he hadn't moved a muscle. My heart beat like a mad thing in my chest. I could feel the heat of him in my belly, like the child we might have had one day. I tangled my fingers in his hair as if that fragile grip would keep him with me.

He shook my hands away and rose to his feet; his eyes were dry now, dry and cold. He kissed me, harshly, hungrily, and pulled the key from my pocket.

"The servants will bring you what you need," he said. I said nothing. The spider sat in her web, frozen as though she herself were prey.

"You will not see me again," he said. The door closed.

Though I listened until my heart stopped, I could not hear the click as the lock tumbled into place.

BATS & BUTTERFLIES

BY CHRISTINE STODDARD

Eleana sits in the English garden, marveling at another Richmond moon, with its clean, clean face (pure at least compared to the jostling James). Her wispy nightgown fans out around her hips like a period costume. A pair of crooked fairy wings hang from her shoulders, shoulders that shine bright white in the glowing night light. Her boyfriend bent the coat hanger she used to construct the wings after she muttered she was pregnant. She wears the ripped panty hose, which she later inundated with dollar-store glitter, the night of the fatal escapade.

Suddenly Eleana stretches out her arms until she can stretch them no farther. They are long and milky before her. Her nails, painted pale gold, twinkle. Eleana draws her hands to her face and breathes in deeply, her chest heaving like a birthing mare's. The scent of lavender lotion mixed with misoprostol emerges from her pores. She shivers.

A massive magnolia overwhelms the garden with the stench of its rotting flowers. The whole tree is dying. Its leaves begin to fertilize the fetus Eleana buried there just as the sun set and shadows started to descend upon the city. She shivers again and sniffs her hands until the stench becomes indiscernible. Eleana inhales the garden's natural perfumes, from waves of Virginia Dogwood to pulses of Tudor Rose.

Eventually, she exhausts her nose. Her ears catch a flicker of sound. Eleana puts her hand over her gloomy gray eyes, shielding the moonlight from her gaze, and looks to the sky. She squints and, a second later, shrieks. Flailing her arms in the midst of wild screams, Eleana finally flings herself to the ground, ignoring the pain of mulch pressing into her soft calves. She rocks back and forth like a cradle. All the while, tears stain her face and she whispers, "I don't know if they're bats or butterflies. I don't know if they're bats or butterflies. I don't know if . . . "

Hours later, the sun rises. The magnolia has shed its final leaf and Eleana's wings lie over her child's grave.

THE SWEET UNKNOWN

BY HARLEY MAY

Dom pulled his cap over his ears to shield him from both the cruel wind and his mother's voice.

"You better not be heading to town," she called as he walked toward the door. "Not with those traps still out there." She put her hands on her round hips, her anger a force in its own right. On the cold wooden floor beneath the table, his two tiny brothers played with tin soldiers. They didn't know anything of work. Not yet.

His older sister stirred a pot of boiling water for their wash. Her eyes mirrored Dom's, sunken and dark underneath.

Dom shook his head, pausing at the door. "Not going to town. I'm going to get the traps, Ma." He left before she could say anything else and made his way to the small dock down the hill. The moment his feet touched the boat floor, his body relaxed. Peace.

Every slice the oars made through the choppy water felt like a prayer of thanks. They took him farther out to sea and away from the two-bedroom house on the hill. He rowed away from the nagging of his mother and into the dark sea. Only one more year and he'd be out of the house. Away from the small fishing town, away from the careful watch of his mother, away from people who saw him as nothing more than a quiet boy.

Away.

Sure, he was shy and kept to himself, but he wanted something bigger. A life that didn't involve smelling like fish. He'd much rather smell like bread. Or books. If he could go away and save for school, that'd be a plan and much better than ending up here.

Dom pulled up alongside the lobster traps as the wind shot through to his bones. With steady hands, he moved the buoy aside and pulled up the trap, one arm-length at a time. It was heavier than normal, harder to pull, and his muscles burned against the dead weight.

Just as his breathing set into a steady rhythm, the trap jerked him forward. Dom wound the rope around his hand an extra loop and tightened his grip as the trap thrashed near the surface. It pulled the rope against his palms, his skin aflame. He wrapped it around his elbow, transferring all the tension to one arm while his free hand grabbed an oar.

While the cage whipped back and forth under the water, he cranked a muscled arm over his head, ready to strike. His shoulder heaved the trap and creature to the surface. The sight of the damage made him stop. The metal stripping was ripped apart by the small seal with her head caught tight in the cage. Metal pressed hard against the black skin, cutting into it, exposing the pink flesh. With her head protected, he couldn't club her out of her misery.

Dom dropped the oar. His hand went to the knife sheathed at his belt. The animal's cries pierced his heart and she thrashed at the side of the boat. As he drew the blade, the seal's scrambling doubled, rocking the boat. He lunged over the edge of the dinghy, grabbed hold of the cage and fell back into the boat. Both the contraption and creature came with him.

They scrambled in a mess in the small boat, tipping it left and right. Dom dropped the knife to steady himself and push the seal off him. He heard the knife slide against the wood to the bow of the boat.

Carefully, he crawled to the knife while she still struggled on the other end of the boat. When he found it, Dom pictured plunging the blade deep into the seal's heart. He steeled his resolve and turned to face her.

What he saw stopped him. The cage lay in shambles on the floor of the dinghy. Small pieces of the seal's skin still rested inside the distorted metal trap while the body of the animal, finally freed, lay writhing at the other end of the boat. The face that stared back at him was not the face of a seal, but a young woman. Dark hair spilled down her fair skin.

A selkie.

"Holy . . . " Blood drained from Dom's face. He shook his head, trying to think the sight away. There she was, a woman, sitting at the other end of the boat. He closed his eyes. Not real. Not real. His eyes opened.

She was still there, squirming in place. His hands gripped the splintered edge of the boat. The impression of her arms and legs moved under the black skin. Her dark eyes darted back and forth between Dom and the sea.

Mesmerized, Dom gazed at her, and the pleading in her eyes brought him forward. With quiet movements, he crept up the length of the boat. Dom was too afraid to blink. Too afraid she'd disappear. He took in the rounds of her eyes, the fullness of her lips, and the lines of worry on her brow.

"Do you need help?" He spoke quietly. Clearly. He didn't want to frighten her. The light creases on her face softened at the sound of his voice. She nodded.

The closer he came, the calmer she seemed. Dom reached for the girl, his hand shaking. He put his hand where the black pelt met human flesh. He moved the dark hair off her shoulders and watched her face, gauging to see if this was what she wanted. Her skin flushed as he moved closer. The outline of her breasts heaved up and down under the seal skin.

He exhaled slowly and ignored the erratic beat of his heart. "I'm going to take the skin off now." It sounded more like a question.

She stared at him and allowed a slight smile. Without a sound, he slipped his calloused fingertips under the seal skin that stopped at her neck. They brushed against her collarbone. Her eyes held his and he pulled on the edges. It stretched and peeled, pulling over the tops of her shoulders. Dom looked back at the girl's face and saw her studying his own.

She nodded, encouraging him to continue.

The skin peeled off her pale flesh like a woman's stocking. It parted perfectly. As Dom neared her breasts, he stopped.

With his hands on either side of her arms, he moved the skin down, exposing her breasts. His fingertips brushed the back of her arms as he pulled, revealing the soft area above her stomach. He watched her breasts rise and fall with her breath. The skin pulled past the dip of her stomach, the curve of her hips, and the top of her thighs. He stopped peeling at the area above her knees, and let his eyes pore over her body. She kicked the remaining black pelt away like a pair of dirty trousers. Dom shifted backward and started to breathe again.

She lay out before him, vulnerable and exposed. Some etiquette in the back of Dom's mind made him look only at her face again while a salty breeze blew over the boat. Her skin prickled in the wind. She shivered and brought her knees up to her chest, hugging them. Dom shrugged out of his pea coat and wrapped it around her thin shoulders.

With their bodies close, Dom noticed a crimson line of blood by her dark hair. He ripped off the cuff of his sleeve and brought it to her head. When he pressed the bit of cloth against the wound, she closed her eyes. After a moment, she took his hand, put her face into his palm, and breathed him in. Her fingertip traced the aggravated pink flesh where the rope had burned him. She put her slightly parted lips on the tender palm. Her hot breath warmed his skin.

Dom cringed in self-consciousness. "They smell like fish. Sorry."

Her lips and nose curled up into a smile. The girl wet her mouth and kissed his palm again. She pulled Dom's hand away in front of their faces.

When Dom looked, he saw that the fresh burn was gone.

She sat there, looking small in his coat, and smiled.

The skin of her legs prickled and purple splotches appeared. He imagined them pressed together under covers. For a moment he saw their lives together—living and making love in a small apartment in the city. He saw her smile every day when he came home.

Her pelt. If he kept the pelt, she'd be his forever. That's what the stories said, at least. In a year he could take her away from here. Away from the village and to the city. Away from the sea.

Away.

But she broke their gaze to look out at the sea. Dom remembered this about the selkies and their legends. She'd always want the water. It didn't matter how she looked at him right now, sitting there in his coat, she would ache for her home later. Dom knew it. Her smile faded with Dom's expression, and he knew she knew. Maybe staying here wouldn't be the worst thing if he could have her.

Dom heard a familiar, nagging voice echo over the cove, calling his name. He turned to make sure his mother couldn't see the girl and felt the warmth of her hands release his.

The boat jostled atop the water. When he turned back around, he saw the points of her toes disappear into the murky deep.

Dom looked back and forth between the shore and dinghy, waiting for the top of her head to come out. He peered over the edge, hoping to catch a glimpse of her, but only found an ache in his heart. Nothing. His pea coat lay on the weathered floor. Her pelt was gone. The waves beat against the edge of the dinghy. He touched where her warm lips had just kissed his palm and stared out into the sweet unknown.

SONG OF SEASONS

BY CANDICE MARIE BROUGHTON

My legs kissed by tulips
Delicate creations
Of complicated beauty
Branches hooked into wet earth
Roots reaching for the sun
Well, what kind of flower are you?
Crystal rain drops on lashes like seeds gestating
And in a moment,
They crash on cheek
Streaks of freshness intermingle with the stale saltiness of petrified
emotion
Artemis's fingers in your hair
Your pigtails the tension in her bow

And I, drunk on golden dust,
Stumbling enough to make Bacchus jealous
Seemingly dancing to the daffodil's song
But it's your nectar that's done me in

The intelligence of youth
The scholastic devotion of memorizing the shape of every leaf
Cataloging each
Noting the change in color
So you won't forget your friends after summer

But in winter,
You won't remember them at all

Until they return in spring in the form of feathers

Pressing flowers in the folds of your skirt
Not knowing their beauty was simultaneously impressing upon you
Pale delight frozen in time
Joy in mimicry
Knowledge in listening
Romance in kissing bark as sap kisses you back
Love spelled out with all the letters between January and July
All the rest left to chance

And I will just buzz by
Only sensing sweetness
Never sensing time
And you
Wondering how a song with no words could have such a complex rhyme
A cat's cradle in a spider's web
All the universe's constellations on a dandelion's head
Freeing a jar of lightning bugs when you hear,
"Sweetie! It's time for bed."

SAY HI FOR ME

BY JOSEPHINE STONE

Dear Tommy,

Listen. I understand that all good things gotta come to an end. I just didn't expect ours so soon.

I know you weren't a big fan of the way I hung out with the guys—Michael in particular. But you know that his dreamy blues couldn't keep me away from you. Or the way that he can always make me laugh, or knows just the song to put on when I'm feelin' down.

Those things wouldn't keep me away from you.

I'm feeling happier now, though. It's been about a week, and I've quit compulsively pressing buttons on my phone to wake up the screen, expecting a new text or missed call while I'm in class. I know you're probably busy.

Baby, I just want you to know that I wasn't distant when Michael was around because he was more interesting or jovial, intelligent or confident. You guys are best friends, and best friends can be so alike. Sure, he'd beat you at all the games and races, including picking me up after work when my car broke down. But who likes a guy who only cares about winning? I just wanted you to know that he had nothing to do with us.

Sometimes I miss when we would hang out. All of us. Hanging out on the porch, laughing at people who walked by, smoking cigarettes and flicking the butts out to the curb. He'd ride up on his skateboard and pop it up into his hand and wave with the hand he'd just brushed the hair out of his eyes with. But you were always the center of my attention, baby. You know that.

Sometimes I wonder if you talk to him about the one that got away the way I do with my friends when I think back to our relationship. And at those moments I wonder if he knows I feel that way.

Well, Tommy baby, I just wanted some closure. Wanted to tie the knot at the end of our frayed friendship bracelet.

Oh, and can you tell Michael I said hello?

OSTRICH

BY NICK CHANDLER

S tifles, fluffing neck to nape
Scheming atlas, heliotrope cities
Road stretch, mix ruff tumble bell
Chime, froth and stumble over
Sweet summer sweater
Trace yarn and candy
Over long lines of pavement
Incumbent, fandangle
Jalopy fuel hounds
Mad happy hyenas
Stalking the bare necks
Of buried-head birds
Bite to find porcelain and polyester
Lace and colored glass
An ocean of milk and sound

WIZARDING LONDON

BY EMILY WAXWELL

T he heart holds the power
in this secretive town.
It's where the Ministry of Magic
breaks queer cases down.

The Ministry of Magic,
full of truth and lies,
is corrupt as any other government,
but that comes as no surprise.

If it's ailments you have,
you might need a visit
to St. Mungo's hospital,
where the cures are exquisite.

To find yourself on the fourth floor
is truly quite bad.
For if that is your location
it's a bad jinx you've had.

Across town lies the Leaky Cauldron,
full of drinks and good cheer.
Its true purpose of existence
is really quite clear.

Push a few bricks down,
and you will find

you have entered Diagon Alley,
where you're truly among your kind.

The street is lined with shops
with knick-knacks of every type.
Visit Ollivander's Wand shop
and you'll find the meaning of the hype.

Wizarding London is a neat place to be,
though it might be just a little bit strange.
Now step onto platform 9 ¾
and watch the world rearrange.

REVERE

BY TINO JUAREZ ━━━━━

Though I may
sound
the trumpet,
or slowly
bang the drum,
the wind it calls your name
much louder.

Tender petals
of your rose
descend their fragrance so
on these,
my banged-up hands.

I swell to see
thee
humble me
so,
I carry multitudes
of kisses
to your mansion.

THE GIANTESS

BY KIRSTY LOGAN

One.
The giantess grows fat on kisses.
She consumes little elfboys
one by one, like bonbons,
pop-popping between her teeth.

She wants you, pretty girlboy.
And she will not wait.

Two.
You will come 'round in your brother's leather
jacket
collar turned up
sleeves covering knuckles.
You will smell of
nicotine and fizzy drinks.
I will be concealed
in silk the colour of tongues.

I will suck the fat
from your lips.

SUN DOG

BY HELEN GEORGIA STODDARD —

A concoction of the rainbow
was blended up today
and thrown into the sky
up amongst the clouds
it hid, peering out
shy little dog
Roy G. Biv knocked on my door
this afternoon
wanted to have a chat
we talked of nature and all things natural
natural dreams of nature filled our mugs
and overflowed onto our saucers
we dipped slices of the moon, sprinkled
with sunshine
into the bitter day
a concoction of the rainbow was blended
up today
and thrown into the sky
up amongst the clouds
it hid, peering out
shy little dog
Roy G. Biv knocked on my door
this afternoon
wanted to come out to play
brought all his toys with him
watercolors and paper
we painted and all the run-off flowed down

the drain
dyeing the world bright
tie-dye, even
a concoction of the rainbow was blended up
today
and thrown into the sky
up amongst the clouds
it hid, peering out
shy little dog
Roy G. Biv knocked on my door this afternoon
wanted to sing some songs
we co-wrote some pieces
put a little guitar here
a piano solo there
we sang and played the greys away
and replaced them with blue skies
a concoction of the rainbow was blended up
today
and thrown into the sky
up amongst the clouds
it hid, peering out
shy little dog
the dog ran away
until a new day comes
we will wait for rainbow splattered skies.

COMING TO TERMS

BY KRISTIAN WHIPPLE

L
ily-white bones
say "I love you."

Porcelain shatters
say "Good-bye."

Webs of lightning—
sizzling hot cracks crawling up my skin.

White roses and raindrops—
purity and peace.

The valley unknown but the mountain icy,
toes sting but bones burn.

You died in a car accident . . .
it wasn't raining.

TODAY I DANCED WITH A SHADOW

BY JOSEPHINE STONE

T oday I danced with a shadow,
taking the lead to and fro.
Today I danced with a shadow,
when I moved high it moved low.
Today I danced with a shadow,
from my doorstep to the church.
Today I danced with a shadow,
it joined me high on my perch.
Today I danced with a shadow,
it pulling the lace of my dress.
Today I danced with a shadow,
as the sun went down it grew less.
Today I danced with a shadow,
'til the night sky touched the earth.
Today I danced with a shadow
that showed me what a day's worth.

AT THE MOMENT

BY MELISSA PALMER

It was hard enough for Josie to get a date these days, what with the economy being so bad. It's not like she could afford to go out to bars, even if she wanted to. It was hard enough with the social networking and the dating sites that promised to find her one-and-only, despite the fact that half of the handsome and available young men messaging her were actually convicts or overweight married guys looking for some kind of treat that had less to do with love and more to do with a tragic spell-check error. It was hard enough with all of that.

And then there were the bagpipes.

She had grown accustomed to the playing, sometimes soft and steady in rhythm with her steps as they fell. But today he was playing louder, more boisterously than usual, an up-tempo number at full volume with little to no pause for breath. When the song was through, he would start it up all over again, the same tune over and over. Normally, her close-walking companion enjoyed changing it up a little, if not for her benefit, then for his own artistic sake, which was why today it was more than just an awkward annoyance to hear the song again and again. A little variation in his song choice, especially at this moment, would be a welcome change from what she'd been hearing on repeat. She was half-hovering under her oversized patent-leather purse, which she was suddenly doubly grateful for having found last week at a consignment shop. It was functioning as more than a necessary umbrella. At this point it acted as her shield, a buffer blocking out the booming sound coming from right behind her.

Some days were easier than others. Some days he'd play the Carpenters or an old Viennese waltz, tunes suited for dentists' offices and discount stores. Other times it was the sweet sounds of the sixties or the more traditional Scottish folk song. Today she wasn't that lucky.

Furthermore, she wasn't doing so well in the getting lucky department.

It's not like she needed a date, not where she was going, but sometimes it would be nice to have someone on a day like this, someone to hold her elbow as she negotiated the slippery sidewalk, ducked under bobbing leaves, heavy with moisture, a nice guy in an overcoat with a large umbrella to keep the cold rain from plastering her hair to the side of her face, and to keep the little black beads of seldom-worn makeup from sliding down her cheeks like solemn skiers.

Stopping before a doorway, she glanced down at the crumpled piece of paper in her hand, which read "3 to 6 P.M." in messy blue handwriting. The ink had begun to run in the droplets that fell from the awning above the entrance, which bore a name in scrolled script. The set of heavy, white wooden doors carved with swirls and squiggles could only mean she was entering somewhere formal, where the only thing colder than the temperature inside would be the small talk and uncomfortably forced smiles.

By the looks of it, she was unfortunately right on time.

"Are you going to stay out here, Fleming?"

The piper, swept away by strains of his own song, finished his tune and looked up somberly as if the question in itself were an offense.

Fleming had gone all out today. His kilt was pressed into perfectly crisp pleats matched exactly by his tunic, which mirrored his bright plaid cross and waist belt. The scheme was quite deliberate. From his Spats to his hose and garters, all the way to his puffed-up feather bonnet, he had made sure every stitch of him was in place, completely squared away. Not one color was off. As far as bagpipers go, he was looking top-shelf.

"I didn't think so," she sighed, taking a moment to straighten the mess that had become her hair, wiping a lone dark skier from her upper lip.

"Here we go."

As expected, a rush of chilled, sterile air brushed her cheeks like an estranged lover's hello kiss. She wished she'd brought a hairbrush or, thanks to the unforeseen downpour, a beach towel to make some sense out of her sodden hair. As if he'd read her mind, Fleming turned up the volume on the song that was now dictating the cadence of her heart.

He was standing close enough to provide her with some much-needed heat at her back. From the front, all she was getting was ice.

An army of eyes shot down the corridor to where she stood, half-frozen by the small room where she'd reluctantly given up her coat. The black and white tiles on the floor suddenly reminded her of a dart board as she trained her stare downward, concentrating on an imaginary shot she needed to make; she would imagine this rather than give any attention to the angry peacock rump that was the group of lovely ladies dead ahead, or to think of how her hair had gone gooey from rain and products she'd never used before.

Fleming was still riffing on the intro to the song. He was adding more flourish and pizzazz this time. He didn't seem to mind that she'd ducked into the bathroom. Bathroom stalls, showers, and other private items of hygienic nature he left just to Josie. It was either out of respect or complete disinterest. She hadn't figured out which yet.

As for her piper, he'd been with her for as long as she could remember. One day in elementary school when the boys and girls were divvying up sides for dodgeball, she'd turned around and there he was, decked out in kilt, tunic, and baseball hat. No one in her class seemed to mind his rendition of "Take Me Out to the Ballgame." By the time she was in high school, folks had just grown accustomed to him, whether he was bleating out "Weird Science" during chem finals or free-styling jazz licks as she sat munching a peanut butter and jelly sandwich at lunch. There was that brief time in junior high when Fleming just up and disappeared. That's when he was suddenly and unexpectedly replaced by a robust and overtly affectionate Gospel singer named Yolanda who was good natured but arguably not Fleming. He was a silent partner, despite the bagpipes. Yolanda was something of an extrovert, bidding praise and advice to all of Josie's schoolmates. It was only then that Josie realized how much Fleming had grown to be part of her. She was thankful when he'd emerged one sunny morning just a couple of years later. Before she could even get out the first word to question what had happened, he'd jumped into a medley of pop songs that were dominating the charts. She appreciated his efforts to be relevant and hip as she got on the school bus for the first time as a high school student. It was somewhere between that day and his soft, seductive rendition of "Killing Me Softly" as she departed for her prom that she stopped questioning at all.

Either way, the warmth of the ladies' lounge was welcome. She loved how these fancy places did everything they could to take something as innocuous and potentially gross as a bathroom and disguise it as something else—a lushly furnished sitting area, an old-timey room full of cabanas. She'd seen a few. This one was set up in toasty mauve velvets. It reminded her of a dressing room she'd see in a saloon in an old western.

No matter; what it was dressed up as made little difference, so long as it served a purpose. The restroom had enough light for her to see the mushy wreck her face had become. How she was convinced to slather this stuff on in the first place now escaped her. She wiped at the mess under her eyes and slicked down her fuzzy, albeit sopping, hair so that she could push some of the stray pieces behind her ears. With her blunt, no-nonsense do half-wet and pushed into submission, she could almost pass for someone who had done her hair this way on purpose, like the models in the old Vidal Sassoon commercials or in music videos with the serious ladies in the black dresses and wound-red lipstick.

It would have to do, this attempt to spruce up for the occasion. It wasn't everyday she met up with her first boyfriend. And it only made matters worse that he'd become obscenely successful in the finance world. Not that Josie begrudged him the success, but it made the crowd even tougher than what she was used to.

The original group of looky-loos had dissipated, leaving behind one or two stragglers who stood agog, looking more like nutcrackers than smartly dressed professionals and suburban soccer moms. She just needed to get down that corridor. It emptied out into a larger room, a more open setup where the pipes wouldn't reverberate in such a way that her bones seemed to shake. It wasn't just in her head. She passed a large glass vase full of flowers that absolutely quaked as they walked by.

"Really?"

She turned back to Fleming with a pleading look as they approached the opening. There were overstuffed chairs on opposite sides of the room. They looked soft, sound-absorbent.

"Can you stop for just one second?"

He looked at her sad eyes and for a moment something happened that hadn't occurred in the past two decades.

He stopped.

At the threshold of the room full of well-dressed people who shook hands, hugged, and pretended to listen to each other, the piper freed his mouth from his music, leaving the room as close to silent as it had been since Josie's conspicuous entrance.

"Thank you," she half-sighed and smiled, touching the small Scot's shoulder. He didn't try to ignore her but wasn't a bit moved by the gesture, too busy with his own business. He steadied his tall, feathered headpiece so it stood perfectly erect, straightened his cross and waist belt that hung against his scarlet tunic like raspberry stripes. He even took a moment to inspect his hose and garters, making sure his legs weren't hiding any stray raindrops or wrinkles. His patent leather Spats looked like mid-life-crisis convertibles gleaming hot in the sun. He made sure he was spot-on before they crossed the threshold.

She didn't see him puff out his cheeks as his lungs filled to capacity. She hadn't guessed that he'd saved his loudest playing for this precise moment.

It was too late. The overstuffed chairs were deceptive, completely lacking any buffer ability. If anything, the loud blasts of "Stayin' Alive" bounced off of the thick leather cushions and ricocheted across the room. The few people who stood in tight clusters loosened up their circles to get a look at whomever or whatever had just made such an entrance. Some looked disappointed that it was only a slightly familiar-looking young woman in brown, slouching so far into her own shoulders she might have been able to pass for headless. They were, on the other hand, agape at the sight of Fleming, who was so engrossed in his own music that it was he who did not notice. Even if he hadn't been putting on the performance of his life, the piper was one often unimpressed and unmoved by the opinions and musings of others. Staring, pointing, even thrown tomatoes were never so much as a distraction, let alone a deterrent for the one who played the pipes.

"Sorry, excuse me, sorry 'bout this . . . it's . . . I can't help what he . . . Oops, excuse me . . . Sorry."

She moved through the path of people that seemed to be carved into the small crowd and continued her apologies to herself, to no one, and to whomever would listen, as she stood in the greeting line.

By the third rendition of the song she could see that he waited there at the end of the line at the far end of the room. He was flanked by women she almost recognized, save one she knew straight out.

She wasn't wearing the traditional white of the perfect catch, but she still smiled the same well-trained, Vaseline-slicked, lifeless grin she'd learned years ago when she was still doing dance recitals and her favorite accessory was a sash.

She was the one who wrote him the letter, the one who said he'd be happier with her and that Josie would understand. It was years ago, petty high school tragedy that meant nothing in the grand scheme of things. It was stupid nothing stuff that was more than under Josie's bridge, but for a split second she thought that Fleming was going to break into a more sinister tune. For a tiny tick, she thought she could hear a beat of something ominous break into the loop she'd forgotten was still going.

People were stopping to talk to her, holding her hands and patting her on the shoulder as she smiled back, nodding, speaking softly, and bowing her head to the one Josie could call her first. He didn't say much. He sat there, reclining, really, with a changeless look on his face. Out of everyone there, he seemed to be the most genuinely at ease.

At least he was happy where he was. She had to believe that.

At least he wouldn't have to deal anymore with the nonsense that she dealt with everyday, the senseless dating anxiety, performing like a circus clown, the pretending, the meeting people and number exchanging, that stupid first-time conversation fodder composed of questions that seem to be pre-written for people. He wouldn't have to act like a game show host or ask the standard twenty questions everyone wants to hear and no one wants to answer, at least not truthfully. He wouldn't have to wonder if he'd be spending his nights alone or get all caught up in that dopiness and romancing that always ends up in some sort of inquiry about forever. Now none of that would be an issue ever again. After today, he'd never have to worry at all.

Josie was glad for him that he had found that peace.

Fleming was booming now, really wailing. Out of the corner of her eye she could see someone fighting the urge to join in on the chorus. Most people are put off by a steady sound track of bagpipes, but she'd been waiting so long in this line that the music had seamlessly become an accepted component of the occasion.

The main squeeze, letter girl, the giant tube of extra-whitening toothpaste, stood there gleaming. Her makeup had been applied expertly, not a hair on her head was out of place. She held a small handkerchief that she apparently did not need in her left hand and blotted at phantom scourges on her face that posed no threat to soiling her cheeks the way Josie's had.

It was interesting to watch her pretend that she couldn't hear Fleming, or better, that she couldn't see Josie approaching, three people back in the line. It was obvious that she could. She'd flinched noticeably only a second ago. But now she was back to nodding at whomever was speaking to her between saintly looks and alternating folding her hands in front of her, then letting them hang serenely at her sides. In down moments, she'd motion to the man next to her or touch his arm or cheek all virtuous and better than everyone in the room. It was her right to act that way, Josie supposed. In a way it was her special day, after all.

Fleming dipped his volume as they approached the head of the line without having to be told or given the pleading look of a person driven half-insane with desperation. Josie gripped at the satin lining of her only business suit. It was brown and utilitarian, but she didn't exactly have a closet full of formal wear, and this was short notice. She squeezed at the jacket lining, pretending to reach for something in an inner pocket that did not exist and attempted to nonchalantly wipe away the clammy layer of cold slick that coated her hands. The song ended. Her time was up. Before Fleming started up again, she cleared her throat.

"Hi, Cherie, you look, uh, good."

Fleming slowed his tempo and quieted into diminuendo.

"I'm, uh, I'm sorry for your loss."

Her smile was fake, but far less strained than Josie had expected. Her well-trained voice was level and even. She could moonlight as a GPS if she ever needed extra cash, though Josie doubted that would ever be the case.

She didn't quite know what else to say to the tanned woman who smiled for no apparent reason. She was fresh from a wedding and even fresher from a honeymoon cut short due to some freak heat lightning and an ill-chosen spot for a siesta.

"Thank you, Josie. How very thoughtful of you to come and pay your," she paused to look at Fleming who was just about sitting piggyback during the exchange, "respects."

"No problem at all." Fleming's music began building again. He'd finished the first chorus at a respectfully slow volume and lullaby's pace, but that reprieve was clearly over. She continued to speak and resisted the urge to raise her voice over the song. No one could compete with the piper when he was charging up, so she leaned in closer than comfort would normally allow.

"I'm not that far away, so it wasn't a big deal to come. So, um, I'm sorry about your honeymoon. And all this."

She had already taken a step back from the casket and the too-soon widow. Fleming was on a roll again, and she had never been a good closer.

"So, okay. Have a good day."

The rain had let up a touch as the duo walked to the economical car that looked more like a small amphibian. Josie's hair stuck out in rusty-brown hunks of hair products and humidity, her suit clinging to her in all the wrong places.

Fleming had let up on the volume so that it faded with the sight of the funeral home in the distance. He sat next to her in the cramped car, looking way too big for the space, even without the feather hat. It sat on the floor in front of him sprouting like a giant red Allium between his knees.

Josie peeled a piece of wet hair from her face and questioned why she'd even gone in the first place.

She looked over at her quiet friend and exhaled a warm breath, her companion shrugging thoughtfully when she spoke the only words to break the silence of the ride home.

"That went better than I'd imagined."

THE FACT CLUB

BY JOSEPHINE STONE

I don't think I'm interested," I said, my hand resting on the bark of the tree's trunk.

It was getting dark and it smelled like it was going to rain, the earth moist in anticipation like freshly cut grass and broken soil.

"I'll bet you are," she said, smiling.

Her eyes turned to half-moon shapes and her lips looked wet. They always looked wet.

Tara finally pulled her right hand from the breast of her jacket to reveal a small, gray kitten.

My eyes grew huge with recognition at my pick of the litter. My grandmother's cat Sandy had kittens earlier in the month and I was set to take Small Gray home in two more weeks. That's what I had been calling him. Small Gray.

"Now how interested are you?" she asked, half laughing.

I started to shake. I knew where this was going. Small Gray was looking down at me from the branch Tara was perched on.

"How 'bout you just cut it out and come back down here?" I said, trying to keep my voice from quivering.

"Yeah? Or what?" she asked, dragging out the last syllable for a couple of seconds.

She began to stretch her arm out, Small Gray dangling from her hand.

"You can't do that," I said.

"Well, you can't be a part of the club then," she replied matter-of-factly.

"What club? Just pass 'im down to me and then we can talk about it down here," I pleaded.

"Uh . . . whoops!" she giggled as she pretended to lose her grip.

Her half moons became crescents while her smile widened.

"The Fact Club. There is always an initiation that's different for everybody. And this is yours," she said.

"Why would I want to be a part of your Fact Club anyhow? Get down here!"

"No! And now you can't make facts. Your words mean nothing. Maybe even the opposite of what you say. Yes—that's it. What I say is fact . . . and I say that what you say is . . . the opposite. That's the rules in Fact Club."

"I don't believe you!" I shouted.

"It's true. I mean, fact. You're not included without initiation," she said.

"Let me have 'im, Tara!" I yelled up.

"So that means you don't want him!" she laughed.

"Cut it out! Stop playing Tara, I mean it. I'll tell Grandma Jean!"

"So you won't tell her?" She burst into a fit of giggles.

"OK. Fine. Keep Small Gray up there then," I said, deciding to play along.

"Is that what you really want, Blake?" she asked.

"Yes. Keep 'im up there with you. I don't want 'im," I said.

"Sure?" she said, crescents growing to full moons, her wet lips reflecting the lights from the house.

"Yes," I said defeated.

"Opposites! Opposites! So that means you're not sure!" she sang.

"No! No is what I meant," I corrected myself quickly.

"OK! Here ya go!"

I watched in horror as Small Gray slipped from her hand, finally making a sound on the way down—a weak, scared meow. He hit the ground with a soft thud, his body rolling over a large root.

I rushed toward his small body, but before I got to my knees I realized he was lying completely still on his back, his legs unmoving.

There was no sound for a minute.

I slowly scooped Small Gray into my left hand and lifted his head with my right pointer finger. His mouth and nose were dripping blood, and his body felt like a small jumble of rocks in a fur pelt, none of the bones or organs where they should be. I didn't know what to do or say.

I cupped Small Gray between my hands, as if to keep him warm, and looked up to Tara with a tear-stained face.

A smile slowly spread across hers.

"Now you're in it!" she shouted gleefully.

I began to shake my head, not comprehending.

"The Fact Club, silly!" she giggled.

There was a loud thud and a crunch of twigs and dead leaves when she jumped down from her branch. I watched her skip up to the house before I fell to my knees, keeping Small Gray closed in my hands.

I laid his tiny body on a curled leaf and covered him up to his chest with another, as if tucking him in. He looked asleep with his eyes closed. Tears dropped from my eyes, wetting his bloody, matted fur. I began to search wildly around with my hands for a stick until I found a thick one behind my feet.

I cried as I dug a shallow grave under the tree for Small Gray, my tears mixing with and moistening the soft dirt next to the root where he met his demise. Still in his leaf bed I moved him to the shallow hole, using a small rock for a pillow for his head.

I began to sob as I pawed dirt and leaves and acorn tops over his inanimate body.

I don't know why, but I began to recite the only prayer I know.

"Now I lay me down to sleep, I pray the Lord my soul to keep . . . "

RAPUNZEL MAN & PRINCESS CHARMING

BY LUNA LARK

In truth, reality's fairy tales are often reversed.
The damsel rescues the bum of a bloke.
Such was the case with Rapunzel Man—no joke.

Sequestered in a tower was Rapunzel Man.
He scratched his buns to pass the time,
among doing one other thing for which there is no rhyme.

Unlike the lovely Rapunzel we all know from the books,
Rapunzel Man lacked something in the department of looks.
He was wrinkled and wiry, and had a beard many yards long.

Oh, what a moping, weeping mess, that Rapunzel Man!
Always hoping to escape! Always keeping to himself!
Lonely and desperate, he had stopped chanting, "I can."

For he could not.
For he would not.
For he should not.

When an evil witch puts a nasty spell on your tower,
you wouldn't dare leave before the final hour,
especially if she told you she'd cut off your prized beard.

Meanwhile Princess Charming with her Nipples of Might
ran through the forest, pursuing her primary delight:
hunting stag with her beloved bow and arrow.

Whilst chasing a thick, red deer one day,
she heard something that interrupted her play.
It wheezed, it coughed, it choked, and it moaned.

No, this was no enchantress' song.
It was Rapunzel Man, rubbing his dong,
unbeknownst to Princess Charming.

In her naivete, she did not find such noises alarming,
but perhaps even a bit disarming,
so accustomed was she to the redundant sounds of stags.

So Princess Charming followed the groans
until she chanced upon Rapunzel Man's secluded tower.
Upon spotting her, oh, how did Rapunzel Man cower!

"Why, it must be the witch in her new form," said he.
"I must pretend I am reading, not performing this blasphemy."
So Rapunzel Man picked up an ancient tome, held upside-down of
course.

"Greetings!" shouted Princess Charming.
"I could not help but notice the strange melodies coming from here.
Were you responsible for such sounds?"

Rapunzel Man blushed and hid his face behind the book.
"Look, Madame Witch, I apologize,
but you must understand how—"

"Witch?" Princess Charming laughed. "You call me a witch?"
Growing nervous, Rapunzel Man began to twitch.
"I do not seek to offend," he said, "But merely to address you properly."

"I am not a witch!" she replied, "I am Princess Charming,
blonde and beautiful, with Nipples of Might,
though, sadly, not the power of flight."

Rapunzel Man jumped. "Have you come to rescue me?"
"I did not know you required rescuing."
"Aye, I do! Please do me a favor and I'll do you three."

"I shall help if I can," Princess Charming shrugged,
"Granted I've rarely proven useless before.
I am all hero, straight to the core."

"Then please, please, please do what you can to release me
from this wretched tower!
So I may rejoice in the natural world, starting with smelling a flower."

Princess Charming assessed the situation,
studying the tower from the ground up.
In two wags of a doe's tail, she saw a lock as round as a cup.

"Simple fare," she muttered to herself.
Then, poising her Nipples of Might,
Princess Charming marched straight up to the lock.

She twisted one of her nipples just like a key.
Suddenly the tower crumbled
and Rapunzel Man was free.

"YIPPEEEEEEEEEE!"
he shrieked with glee.

"Now what about those favors?" Princess Charming inquired.
"Well," Rapunzel Man paused, "What is it you require?"

From then on, Princess Charming had just the fellow
to gag and bellow until the stags
emerged from the woods in curiosity.

BROTHEL WITHOUT A HEARTBEAT

BY JOSEPHINE STONE

I look at the layers of rock. The ones on top are light and look like they are covered in powder. As I dig deeper with my plastic ladle, the rocks beneath are darker, clumped tight together and heavy. In some corners, it is easy to wedge the spoon under a clump at a forty-five degree angle and lift it out, sending smaller rocks spraying across the wood floor. These bigger clumps are the spots where she likes to urinate. The feces are easier to get out. They are always on top, and she usually does a good job of covering them so they just slide onto the spoon and into the wrinkled, plastic grocery bag. Good cat. You have me whipped, Skaldskaparmal, and sometimes I cannot believe I get on my hands and knees to sift through these layers of disgusting pebbles, actually thinking to myself about igneous, sedimentary, and metamorphic layers of your shit and piss. You are my best friend, though, and I suppose people do a lot for friendship sometimes.

I'm already late for work, and that makes me relax. It's the initial hitting the time you're supposed to be there that's a doozy. Might as well take a nap now. I shake my head at my lethargy and figure that if I've already had my face in Skalds's box, my day can't get much worse. It's not much work to do anyhow, just a few visits to make before I contact Rob with the stats. I throw on my best black suit, walk through each room to make sure all of the lights are off, and then head out to catch the bus. I kind of like the fact that it is so unreliable, and that everyone looks so sad on the bus. It's like we're on a ride to visit our terminally ill children, or to a gas chamber, and the driver knows it and doesn't want to hurry because none of us really want to get there too fast. People always seem to be thinking so hard, too, and it can be suffocating at times.

I hop off at the Cranston Street stop across from a strip mall with its basic chain grocery store, Chinese restaurant, alcohol store, and tattoo shop. I stay on the east side of the street and walk up the asphalt to the door of Moore's Funeral Home. Thankfully there are a lot of cars out front, a good sign. I am glad a lot of people are here to see her, and it will take the pressure off of me having to talk to anyone. I walk in and hear the typical, drab piano music playing from a hidden boom box. The place is packed, the walls covered in flowers. I take a seat in the back row, preferring to walk up alone, or when there is less of a line. I'm one of those wait-till-all-those-pushy-people-board-the-plane, or get-lunch, or get-into-Wal-Mart-on-Black-Friday kinda guys. I can wait.

Approximately an hour of people-watching passes before I head up to see her. I try to look solemn, but it's hard around all these really bad hats and sandals. I can't believe some people. I see her, pretty as a picture with her hands crossed under her breasts. Her long, auburn hair is neatly combed and she is wearing a white dress her parents picked out. She looks so alive it's surprising when her hands don't rise and fall with breath or beating heart. I crouch down as if to tell her something, and just stare at her face, perfectly preserved. She is much more pale than in her obituary, but is still the stunning shell of a twenty-three-year-old woman taken too soon. I try to make a face I imagine someone who just had a great deal of closure would make, and walked back through the wake and into the sunlight. Time to catch that shiny monster downtown.

I get off at the 22nd Street stop this time and walk a few blocks over to Samson Avenue where Rob's building is. It's located in an industrial warehouse area that is mostly empty and is one of many eye sores that line the block. For cheap, he has a few floors and a large basement. His office is on the first floor. I ring the bell and stand where the camera can see the back of my throat as I pretend to consume the small "hidden" piece of equipment.

"Knock it off, asshole," Rob seethes through the slits of the intercom located right above the bell. "Get in here."

The door buzzes and I walk in straight down the hallway toward the back. His office is the only open door, and the only light on. His building is always so cold and so dark inside. I plop down on a crumb-covered arm chair in front of his desk and cross my left leg over my right. I can hear a guy moaning through the wall in the room right next to us and I grimace.

"Is that Thomas?" I ask, annoyed, staring at the groaning wall.

"Nah. Some new guy. He's cool. If you wanna check out the sitch, it's a new one, too," Rob replies as he continues to type and stare at the computer screen.

I exhale a deep breath while I uncross my legs, as though I am doing him a big favor. I slap my hands on my knees and push up. The chair creaks. My dress shoes echo on the green linoleum floor, and I slowly turn the knob of the next door over. I put my head through the crack I have made without opening the door much further. I don't want much light to get in, or for this new guy to notice. The room has no windows and there is a bed in the middle. A young, pale guy is violently thrusting his hips between the open legs of a girl, panting and repeatedly picking her leg back up to rest against his side. I quickly close the door.

"Looks good," I say once I'm back in the room. "But you need to see the beaut from today. About 5'7", 120 pounds, auburn hair."

"Oh, the tragic drug overdose?" Rob asks sarcastically, still occupied and still sounding as though he isn't really listening or caring.

"Yeah. She's great. She'll be at Greensburg tonight. Joanna should be there," I mumble, picking lint off my shirt.

"Per-fect," Rob says with the last two slams of the enter key.

He turns his chair finally to face me.

"Well, don't you look nice today," he smiles.

I shake my head. This is the part where I should blush and say, "Aww, you cut it out." But I'm not buying into those weird games. I hate when he looks so smug, complimenting me as if I just learned how to dress today or just showed him how I used the toilet instead of the small, pink chair next to it. I am not his child.

"What time are you thinking we head down?" he asks, realizing my annoyance isn't topical.

"Joanna said two. Should be enough time," I reply.

The moaning stops. We looked at each other. We hear the door open a few moments later and the young man appears in the door frame of the room we're in, his distorted shadow thrown across the floor like an oil spill, or what I imagine a demon would look like. His face is sweaty, and he looks embarrassed that I'm here.

"This is Dave," Rob says to the young man, pointing at me. "And this is Steven."

We both mumble "nice to meet you"s and don't shake hands, for good reason. Steven, looking nervous, pulls out a wad of cash in a rubber band and sets it on the desk.

"We're meeting tonight, and you're more than welcome," Rob says with a smile as he pulls the wad closer to his side of the desk.

"Yeah, uh, thanks. I, uh, have to work tonight at the . . . " Steven says as he points his thumb awkwardly over his shoulder.

"At the pizza shop. I know. But if anything comes up, just stop by," Rob says with a larger smile. He likes knowing things about people and reminding them that he knows at random times. He's a freak.

Steven starts to turn on his heel. I nod at him and he's out the door.

"What is that kid, like eighteen?" I ask, raising my voice when I hear the front door slam.

Rob shrugs and lights a cigarette.

"You mind?" he asks as he points to the now-silent wall, blowing the smoke out of his nostrils.

I let out another deep breath, slap my knees, and am back in the room. It smells sick, like old food and semen. The girl lies on her back, in the same position I saw her with Steven. When I get closer to her face, I gag.

"ROB! ROOOOB, GET YOUR ASS IN HERE!" I yell through the wall.

A moment later he's behind me.

"The kid fuckin' mutilated her," I say angrily. "He pay extra for this? 'Cause we can't use 'er again now."

The girl's eye sockets are swollen and pooled with blood. Between her blue, split lips, broken teeth can be seen blocking the back of her open throat. It's obvious her cheek and jaw bones are broken, her face unstructured, unshaped, inhuman. Her breasts and thighs are covered in bruises whose color bleeds into intricate spider-web-like designs of dark purple and blue. The carnage reminds me of a squashed squirrel I saw during a stroll through a residential area yesterday, its guts pushed out through its mouth, completely flat like a spent bottle of toothpaste.

"Yeah. Forgot to tell you about this new deal I've come up with," he says, pulling the blanket over the girl's face. "In addition to our new option of price variance based on levels of dec-, er-, on levels of freshness, I figured we could get people to pay extra for the chance to do whatever they want to the body. You have no idea how many sadists in this town are going to eat this special offer up!" he finishes with a toothy smile.

I stare at the blood soaking through the sheet covering where her face had been.

"Whatever, man. I don't know if I'm really cool with—"

"And does what you're cool with matter at all in this situation? You are a grunt. You are the one on the hunt. You are completely replaceable," Rob says before I can finish my sentence.

I let out another deep sigh as I begin pulling the sheets from under the mattress and flipping them over onto the top of the bed. I grip the corners of sheets at the head of the bed and stare over at Rob, my mouth drawn in a tight line.

"You helpin' or what?"

He takes his place at the foot of the bed and grabs each corner. We lift at the count of three and make small shuffles with our feet, biting our lips at the weight and strain on our arms. There's a small square door located in the middle of the wall in the hallway, probably once used for a dumb waiter, or for a trash disposal for a furnace in the basement. Rob drops his end of the load with a thud and pulls the handle of the small trap door open, groans as he bends over to pick her back up, and then we watch as the bottom of the white sheet flutters into the darkness of the hole. We stand there listening for the slam at the bottom, smiling at each other, and exaggeratedly brush our hands off for a job well done.

"I'm headin' home. Be back around two for the pick up," I say, still wiping my hands off on my black slacks.

"What about preparations for the meeting tonight? It'll surely be over by then," Rob says with an air of disappointment. "You would get to see all the guys, all the new girls set up, have some drinks."

"I'll show up early. But I'm not helping you set up some fag fest. I'll be back around midnight, I suppose."

I begin to slowly walk down the hall, feeling his eyes burning into my back. He doesn't like when I decide what I'll be doing, but I'm not going to be his bitch tonight. I spend every day doing that.

Once at home, I plop down on the couch and grab the shoe horn on the side table.

"Skaldskaparmaaaal, guess who's hooome!" I say in as cheerful a voice as I can muster. I always feel anxiety before these meetings, before the pick-ups, before schmoozing with the scum that partakes in the furnace I fuel. A small cat on my lap usually helps with the unwinding.

"If you don't come out now, I'll never point a laser at the floor in this house agaaaiiin."

Still no reply. My best friend is very fickle, very unreliable, and not very punctual. We are so similar. I smile thinking about how I'd treat me the same way if I were her.

I wedge my shoes off with the horn and moan with relief. Those damn dress shoes strangle and scrape the back of my foot, and I have been able to feel my heart beat in my heels all day. After pointing my toes and rolling my ankles in small circles with my eyes closed and head laid back against the wall above the couch, I get up and walk over to the desktop computer in the corner of the room.

Minesweeper—the next best thing to small Skalds. Fuck her, I think to myself. I'm about to be tiptoeing 'round some bombs, causin' that emoti-con to show me his "O-face" with each click.

After five successful guesses the smiley face's eyes turn to X's. I killed him. I stare at the screen and begin to think of how quickly that happened.

How this silly game can say so much about the quickness with which death can be served. It's a wonder I can have some existential moment about the brevity of it all when I deal in death. My sensitivity at times makes me want to vomit. I decide to call Joanna.

"Greensburg Morgue."

"Hi, this is Dave. Was wondering if Joanna was on duty today."

"Um, sure. Hold on a sec."

I can hear the phone being set on the counter, the rumble of the spiral phone cord moving against the receiver and a muffled "Joannnnaaa!" from the woman's voice on the other end. A few seconds later, I hear light breathing on the other end.

"Hi Dave," Joanna says. Her voice is sweet and she sounds twelve over the phone.

"Hello, my crust puppet. Just wanted to check in."

"Oh, how nice to hear from you, my little broken bulb."

She's good at playing along with my games, knowing exactly why I'm calling, and adding to the fun of quickly coming up with silly pet names on the spot. We don't need any fuckin' Sudoku to work these circuits.

"So the eagle's still landin' at two?" I ask, deepening my voice to sound like a commander on a secret mission.

"Cut the crap, Dave. I'll be back here then, and if you're late, I'm gone. We won't have much time. I'll have the cameras off, the files gone. It'll be fine. Just got in some unidentified cremated remains that'll do. If you keep calling me like this you'll have my coworkers unconvinced that I'm a lesbian. Gotta go."

I sigh at the click and, after slowly dragging the phone down my ear and neck, I swing it up into my palm and onto the receiver. My only friends are people I work with, ones who would never call me their friend and always just want to keep things strictly business. Joanna has been working at Greensburg for years. I met her at a Waffle House one morning at four A.M., shortly after Rob and I came up with our genius plan for the brothel without a heartbeat. Her occupation was pure serendipity. Rob and I had been friends for several years, met back in college, and since then had always been working on crazy business schemes like no-touch bathroom stall doors, pizza gum, and meals with feels. Our latest venture was proving to be the most profitable. He is the brains, the organizer, and I am the outside man, the supplier. We collect corpses from Joanna, preferably Joe and Jane Does, homeless or without families. Age, race, cause of death are all unimportant, but each caters to different clients, and depending on supply and demand, directly affects price. The business of cremation has been booming, with corpses reserved for funeral services becoming less and less common, so we've begun delivering, with a sum of money, the cremated remains of random objects and animals for Joanna in order to get the cream, or, really, the corpse of the crop. We provide discounts depending on levels of decay and the amount of times a body has been used. Sometimes, in rare situations, the higher the number, the higher the price for the sickest clients. After doing this for a couple of years, we can read what a guy wants in a matter of seconds, by his body language, his wandering eyes, his perspiration. I am the magic eight ball of these men's fantasies, and with one shake of a hand can pinpoint and price a client.

I look at the floor and Skalds is on her back, twisting and wriggling her body on the soft carpet with her feet folded in submission on her chest, reminding me of mosquito larvae in standing water.

"Now that you've decided to show up, I'm leaving."

I head up the stairs to the small bedroom located at the top. I change into jeans and a button-up long-sleeved shirt and slip my feet into some running shoes. I want to blend in, as much as that is possible, with this group of men who will be seeing the Betties Rob is setting up in each room. Presentation is key, especially when gaining new members. I think sometimes about how these are men from all over the neighborhood. Men you think look normal as they walk their Labrador through the park, as they use the microfilm lamps in the library, as they talk you into the 40" TV set at Best Buy, or, as in Steven's case, as they deliver your pizza. I guess it's sort of like finding out the president of the PTA at your child's school is a member of the NRA. Or that the old man across the street who sits in a lawn chair waving at traffic is a registered sex offender.

I have time to kill, so I lie back on top of the covers of my made bed and set an alarm on my phone for 11:30.

• • •

I am grateful Rob's building is in a secluded area of town when I can hear voices inside from across the street. I ring the bell and position my face centered in front of the camera. The door buzzes. The solitude from earlier today is completely absent, each room full of people, smoke, clinking glasses, and chatter. The first door on the right is a large living room where most of the guests are congregated and where Rob notices me immediately.

"Everyone. Everyone! This is my partner, Dave!" he shouts above the dull droning of voices.

Most turn to look at me, some smile, some wave, some say, "Hello, Dave," "Nice to meet you, Dave," "Thanks for having us, Dave." I do not make an effort to smile, but do make one to get to a corner of the room with a chair where I can sit, avoiding eye contact with anyone who might want to talk or ask me a question. I, like most here, am just here for the tour of the new ladies—and to get directions before picking up the new one from Joanna. A lot of the men around the room are middle aged, gripping the necks of their beer bottles as if they were live animals, anxious of their escape. Rob can tell by my expression that I do not wish to be here long and begins the formalities.

"Most of you know of our facility, and the business we provide. For new clients, you will soon know. We do not have these meetings regularly, but when a larger shipment is made or when a larger amount of members exist, we find it necessary to clean the place up and present, celebrate, and guide," Rob said with pride. "This is the first floor, and it has five rooms. The second and third floor each have seven. Any room can be designed to fit personal taste and preference, and décor generally rotates to keep things new. Same with the women who work the building, and for good reason," he said, as the knuckleheads around the room all laughed. "Let's take a look."

He swings his arm in the air open handed, gathering invisible gnats or ghosts, orchestrating the group to follow him into the next room down the hall. Every other room of the building is significantly smaller than the living room, so a few men can step in and look, while others peer over shoulders, nodding and grumbling. I keep my distance, waiting to see each room after all have passed. The first room contains the perfectly preserved corpse of an older school teacher who died in a car accident. She is lying on the bed, eyes closed, arms crossed, in a school teacher costume. The gray wisps of her hair curl as if she had been awake before our arrival, primping for her exhibition. Next to each door there is a box of numbers for interested clients. This number serves as a bid for the body.

The next room has a young woman chained by her wrists to the wall, her head down with her chin on her chest as if she's found a comfortable enough position to fall asleep while bound in such a predicament. Another room has an older black woman who's missing a leg, sprawled out in the middle of a large bed, dressed in a glitter mini skirt and a black lace bra. The last two rooms are empty. Rob's office is the last one in the hall.

As we move upstairs, the more bizarre the set ups become. One room is set up with a woman to look like a back room of a masseuse parlor, one room glimmers like a discotheque, another has films playing on the walls of women walking around the street, strange voyeuristic shots of innocent moments of their day. Somehow we've been lucky to get a great deal of younger ones, and I can tell the guys are impressed.

"I remember reading about her, and how she was one of the only people in the state to die from the flu this year," a tall man with a hat says to another.

"Someone told me that the one-legged woman on the first floor lost it to gangrene," replies another.

What the fuck is wrong with these guys? I think to myself. I wonder why they don't go to where they can have real women. Where half of the rooms don't have a suffocating stench. Rob and I will have to make sure to rush around to get all these ladies in the walk-in fridge in the basement after closing up, because they don't last long out on parade like this.

At the third floor, Rob unveils his new violent brain child. Weapons line the walls of each room. There's a medieval room with maces and armor, a more hands-on room with razor blades and ropes, and a modern room with cauterizing tools and trays of shiny metal knives and hooks. I can't believe he only told me about the idea earlier today and already has a full setup. Usually these rooms look like the silly ones on the lower floors. I can't believe how fast the numbers go on this floor. The men now each have one or two. Rob moves up to the front of the crowd, calls each out in order, and the highest bidder receives a key and permission to be excused. Soon each door is shut, with some guys waiting in the hallway on benches making awkward conversation and perspiring.

"Don't look at me like that," Rob says, knowing I'm annoyed with the setup of the third floor.

"You didn't even ask my opinion, and now it is a concept with its own floor! I really don't have a say on what goes on here. Fuck this place."

I turn and start down the stairs, half expecting him to tell me to stop, to wait up, for him to apologize for his rash behavior without my consent. The sound of my footsteps punctuates the silence as I make my way to the front door.

Joanna will console me. She's good at that. I am looking forward to being surrounded by the artificial air of the fridge units that pull out like shelves all around the wall. Her hands coated tight with latex. The lab coat and name tag. She has the face of an angel, the job of an undertaker, and the scheming mind-set of a villain. All of this generally confuses and excites me. How can she be a part of all this, when she is like that? I can see my breath shoot out in large plumes from my mouth as I cross the empty street and get into my car. I sit for a minute looking at the front door, wondering if he'll appear in its frame to catch me. I turn on the ignition and pull away toward the interstate.

TAKE THE SECOND LEFT ON YOUR RIGHT

BY MICHAEL C. KEITH

He is lost to the forest."
— Sir Walter Scott

Navigating the narrow, one-way streets of downtown Boston required a host of virtues, foremost among them patience. It was not a personality trait Emil Clayton possessed. This was never more evident than when he was behind the wheel in heavy traffic or, even worse, when he was lost. He would quickly lose it and curse everything in his path, especially drivers that were elderly or female. His wife, Carla, had experienced his outrages countless times and dreaded them. He was impossible to placate in this frenzied state. Carla would try her best to tune him out, but she was seldom able to do so.

On numerous occasions she had made clear her displeasure with his over-the-top behavior, but it only intensified his ire, resulting in a nasty shouting match and a prolonged period of icy silence when all was said and done. The experience was all too familiar, and Carla had finally reached the end of her tether.

"No more! I can't take you going ballistic like this. It's scary. You really have some anger issues."

"Only when I have to deal with idiot drivers and the medieval streets in this frigging city," protested Emil.

"Get over it. You've been like this since we got married. You'll have a heart attack. You should see yourself. Your face is contorted and veins pop out of your temples. You look psycho. Doctor Jekyll and Mr. Hyde," replied Carla disgustedly.

Stung by her comments, Emil began to calm down. "I know. I'm sorry. I just lose it," he said.

His meltdown was always followed by a period of remorse and self-loathing.

"No kidding. I'm so tired of it. You say this after every explosion, and then it happens again and again," Carla said.

Emil had little to offer in his defense. He had to agree that in his driving behavior, he was a jerk—there was no getting around it. As usual, he sank into a dark funk over his indefensible behavior. No further words were exchanged until his hangdog expression diffused his wife's displeasure.

"I think you have to remind yourself about how crazy you become when you're in traffic or lost. Maybe you should get one of those GPS things," Carla offered.

"I don't know," replied Emil grimly.

"My brother loves his."

"Your brother is a gadget freak. He buys anything new."

"GPS devices are hardly new. Many drivers use them. You really need to get one so you don't stroke out."

"I'll think about it," muttered Emil.

"Get one. I can't put up with this any longer. If you don't, I'm not riding with you into town any more."

"I'll see," replied Emil, as he parked the car next to the restaurant where they had a reservation.

"What do you know, we're ten minutes early after all your freaking out about being late," observed Carla sarcastically.

Embarrassed, Emil attempted to redirect his wife's justifiable harangue, but he failed and they shared few words over dinner. The ride home was no more animated.

Shit, this frost will last for a while. I better look for a used GPS on eBay, thought Emil. If he could get one cheap, he would buy it to get back in the good graces of his wife. The idea of actually using it, however, did not really interest him.

• • •

Emil finally did go online to find a previously owned GPS. For $50 he purchased a "like new" Tom-Tom. But true to form, it remained in its package until Carla pressed him to put it in his vehicle.

"For heaven's sake, try it out. You might actually like it," grumbled Carla, while her husband held it gingerly like a dirty diaper. "We can use it on our trip."

It was just two days before they were to travel to upstate New York to pick up a Golden Retriever puppy from a breeder as a replacement for their longtime beloved dog that had died a few weeks earlier. Then, the day before they were set to go, Carla twisted her knee and could barely walk, so it was left to Emil to fetch their new pet.

"Make sure you use the GPS. By the time you get back, you'll be an expert with it," said Carla, applying an ice pack to her injury.

Emil had read up on the device and actually found himself somewhat intrigued by it.

"It is a pretty neat thing," admitted Emil, to his wife's considerable satisfaction.

"Well, listen to you, Mr. Luddite," she responded with an approving smile.

"I'll see if it really knows the way," said Emil, readying himself for what he estimated to be a four to five hour drive.

"Be careful," said Carla, lying on the couch with her afflicted leg elevated, as Emil blew her a kiss.

"You be careful, too. Watch that knee. I'll be back tonight with the puppy," answered Emil.

He had programmed the GPS according to the manual but forgot to turn it on until he was on Route 95.

"Take a right onto the Mass Pike ahead two-thirds of a mile," instructed a pleasant female voice from the dashboard-mounted instrument.

"Will do, sweetie," replied Emil. "Hope you know where we're going. You chicks aren't famous for your sense of direction. Maybe you got a guy there to help you?" he asked, half-jokingly—allowing a second to pass before answering his own question. "No? Well, I guess I'm at your mercy, so lead the way."

• • •

The voice on the GPS had sounded familiar to Emil from the moment he heard it, and halfway to his destination, he realized why. It possessed the vocal qualities—or more succinctly the lack of any distinctive vocal qualities—of a college girlfriend he had jilted long ago. After five months of what had become a tempestuous relationship with her, Emil had met the woman who would become his future wife. When he informed his girlfriend that he was ending their rocky union, she threw a tantrum and tossed a wine glass at him. It had narrowly missed his face. Yet her outbursts didn't end there. Three days later she accosted him at the student union trying to heave a cup of hot coffee at him. Fortunately, she dropped the steaming brew before she could launch it at him.

For two months she stalked him, but only once had she made actual contact with him. It was to ask if they could hook up again for one last date. "Just a farewell fuck," was how she had put it. Emil explained that he was now in a committed relationship, and she responded by telling him that it would never be over between them—that someday he would be hers again. After that he spotted her a couple more times—once spying on him from behind a tree and another time walking across the snow-covered campus in his direction. He had retreated into a dorm to avoid her.

A year passed and then he heard that she had dropped out of school. He was relieved by the news, but wondered if he had been the cause of her departure. As time passed, however, she finally faded from his thoughts. Until now, that is.

"Turn right at exit 41," directed the GPS.

"Hey, Sabrina . . . Sabby. Long time no hear . . . fortunately. How've you been all the years?"

"Continue for eighteen miles . . ."

"Ever find happiness? I mean, find someone who could put up with you. You were pretty daft, so if you did, he probably dumped you, too."

Emil continued talking to the GPS. It entertained him and made the time pass quickly. It was also nice to vent at an approximation of someone who had briefly made his life a misery.

"Think you were the type that would find some poor unsuspecting jerk to marry you and get you pregnant. Then you'd murder your family while they slept."

"Take the second left on your right," advised the Sabrina-like voice on the GPS.

"Huh?" muttered Emil, confused.

"Take the second left after the next right."

"Oh, that makes more sense. Guess I heard you wrong," said Emil.

He followed the directions but was perplexed when the second left turned out to be a dead end. He reset the GPS, and it instructed him to drive north to Route 31 west.

"I'm losing my patience with you, but we've been there before . . . haven't we, Sabby?" remarked Emil, as he drove out of the cul-de-sac.

• • •

As Emil cruised along Route 3 toward Gouveneur and the puppy that awaited him, he was caught up in the beauty of the Adirondack Mountains that surrounded him. It was a place he had spent part of a summer with his parents as a child, and he was glad to return. The GPS voice broke his reverie.

"Take Route 56 north one mile."

"Right-oh, Sabby. Your wish is my command," replied Emil.

When the time came to change roads, Emil was surprised to find himself on a single lane blacktop without a centerline.

"Hope you're right about this, old gal," said Emil, as he sped down the desolate strip of asphalt edged on both sides by encroaching woods.

Half an hour later, Emil became concerned by the total absence of any human presence.

"Take the next left at McComber Road," directed the GPS.

In less than a mile, he reached the turn, which consisted of little more than a gravel path just wide enough for a car.

"Whoa, Sabby. This can't be right. Where the hell you taking me?"

Emil pulled over and fished a map from the glove compartment.

"No offense, but I'm going to check a more reliable source . . . Mr. Rand McNally," said Emil, unfolding the New England road guide. "There's Route 56 . . . Crap, the damn map only shows a piece of it," grumbled Emil. "Should have brought along a New York State atlas."

"Continue ahead for three miles to Route . . ."

Several moments of silence followed.

"Yeah? To Route what?" blurted Emil, his frustration mounting.

No answer came, and when he tried to reset the GPS, its function was unresponsive.

Great! No GPS and no map. I'm screwed, thought Emil, who then decided to drive on, hoping he would reach the unidentified route.

He drove well past the three miles the GPS had indicated before he considered turning around. The road was so narrow and the brush so thick on either side that he could find no place to attempt a roundabout. He had no choice but to follow the road wherever it led, and Emil began to wonder if it led anywhere.

"Take the second left on your right," instructed the Sabby-like voice of the digital navigator.

"Not that shit again, you crazy bitch!" snapped Emil, tightening his grip on the steering wheel.

Then the road divided.

"Take the second left on your right," repeated the GPS.

"What the . . . ? Okay, I'll stay right and look for a second left," he muttered, desperately.

Sure enough, there appeared a second road to the left, and it was only a few yards beyond the first turn. By now the sun had set, forcing Emil to follow the beams of his headlights.

"Continue ahead," instructed the GPS over and over as Emil's apprehension grew exponentially.

Again, he considered turning back, but there was no doing so. The road was even narrower than the one he left a few miles back. Tree limbs reached from the sides and scrabbled against his car. Emil feared the road would eventually constrict like a clogged artery, making it impossible to move forward.

Back up. Get the hell out of here, he thought, but when he put the car in reverse, he found he had no back-up lights.

"Jesus," he whined. "This can't be happening."

"Continue ahead," directed the GPS, and Emil hit the off switch.

"You douche bag!" he bellowed.

"Continue ahead . . . continue ahead," repeated the GPS, despite having its power cut.

Get out and walk back to the main road, Emil told himself.

To his horror, he found the doors of his car held tightly closed by the impenetrable wall of trees.

"No," he whimpered and pressed the accelerator.

The car would not move in reverse, so he jammed it into drive and it lurched forward. For another twenty minutes, Emil drove in the only direction he could while the GPS urged him on.

"What the hell is going on?" repeated Emil, on the verge of sobbing.

His dread was compounded when the gas gauge warning light came on.

"I'm trapped! I'm fucking trapped!" he howled. He then spotted a light in the distance. "Oh, thank God!"

He pressed the gas pedal as far as it would go, not caring that it caused the tree limbs to bump against his car. He could not have cared less if the car was damaged beyond repair as long as he could get out of his untenable situation. All he wanted was to reach civilization and end his nightmare.

As he approached the lighted structure, the GPS declared that he had reached his destination. Before him in a small clearing was a pristine dwelling adorned in flower boxes. It reminded Emil of the cottage in Hansel and Gretel.

Is this the kennel? Emil wondered. He stopped the car and surveyed the area. There were no fences or signs of a dog run. The perfectly groomed landscape suggested it was an unlikely place for dogs to be raised and trained. It did not resemble any kennel he had seen.

"You have reached the end of the road," declared the GPS.

"The end of the road is right," Emil mumbled, deciding to inquire within about his location and get directions.

I'll never go back that way, he promised himself . . . *never.*

He climbed the steps of the porch that led to the front door and rang the bell. In the distance he heard the chimes sound the first few notes of

Bach's "Abide With Me." The door slowly opened, and before him stood the last person he ever wanted to see again.

"I knew you'd find your way back to me," said Sabrina, her arms out-stretched in greeting.

Only she could hear Emil's anguished cry . . . and that pleased her.

THE WOODS

BY SYLVIE BEAUVAIS

When the battle-hardened warrior we ironically call Little Red Riding Hood spoke to me, I had to notice that I'd been lied to. She is really tall and slightly menacing, sword at her side. She slouches and leans sideways to talk, but as soon as she's not dealing with peers, superiors, or press like me, she stands straight and has that determined, efficient walk found in athletes and trained soldiers.

She could be pretty if she weren't so damn scary looking. She stared me down for a moment, as if she were evaluating how much I would slow her down when the battle started. Her eyes were startling, so clear and purple blue, like a falling night, that I looked away to see her scar, like a deep, long dimple, on the left side of her face.

"Miss Hood?" (No one knows her real name except the Queen.)

"Call me Red."

"All right, Red. How long have you been in the Army?"

"A few years."

"What made you join the Night Corps?"

"I like to run at night, always have, figured it would be safer if I had a pack with me."

This was an insufficient explanation for going through the most badass training possible. So I pushed her.

"And the killing?"

"I'm here for the mission—I like to get things done right, fast, and quiet."

"Since we can't discuss your next assignment, what can you tell me about your last mission?"

"Special duty. I was to deliver a payload to a rendezvous point. Things didn't quite work out the way I hoped. Lost my crew. Got ambushed."

"And then?"

"A Cleaver Unit was called in for rescue."

My quizzical expression gave me away. She shook her head, stared me down.

"I thought you had clearance."

"I have full clearance."

"And you've never heard of the Cleaver Unit?"

"As I told you, you're my first assignment. They shortened my training to get me into the field fast."

She stared at me.

"This interview's not going well. What would you like to talk about?" I felt a little desperate.

"Why don't you follow me for a bit? I need to get out of here. Back in the Woods."

"Sure. I'll get my stuff . . . "

"No need. We've got standard issue packs—that's all you'll need. What's your running pace?"

"Six minute mile."

"That'll do. Let's go."

I felt a surge of excitement. Holy shit. Outside with Red. When I got the assignment, I was excited. But even my fantasies weren't this wild. She took a side door and we walked quietly down a long, dark corridor to the supply room. She handed me a pack and picked up a bow and some silver-tipped arrows. It was late, the night patrols were already out, the room was quiet, cluttered, full of weapons lockers; it smelled like sweat, fear, and metal.

"Show me your boots."

"They're standard issue."

"Good. Ready?"

"Ready."

I was wondering if we should be checking in with anyone, getting clearance before leaving Vindolanda, but I'd already signed a release, and if I was going out, well, I would never be safer than with Red.

She punched a code into the door lock. We went into a decon chamber, were cleared and then the door opened to the Woods.

The Woods. I had never been. I had been to the forests in the municipal parks, but they don't serve ice cream and caramel popcorn in the Woods.

The Woods were like nothing I had ever seen. Everything was thick and dense, leafy, with hanging vines. A few narrow paths existed, but those paths were shared by people and werewolves alike. There wasn't much room to maneuver, or defend yourself, as the paths were carved among the tall brush. Whatever little light there was came down into the trees and was reflected among the Old Ones. The oldest of the trees known to man, they had grown thick and tall. I wondered why they weren't called the Silver Ones, since their bark transmitted light. We ran in a file among the trees, and the Woods were loud, noisy with life. I could feel small, sharp-toothed, creatures whenever we paused, trying to get through my boots to my toes.

I felt wary and weird. The Woods made it clear that humans weren't wanted. I supposed that was part of the ancient enchantment. The enchantment that had pushed the humans back to the prairie lands called Vindolanda, the enchantment that had created the werewolves during the first war. The werewolves whose purpose was to hunt the humans and keep them out of the Woods.

"Why are we out here?" I wondered out loud.

"We have a mission," said Red.

"A mission?"

"Yes, an important mission."

"To do what?"

"We're going to find the Grand Mother. And we're going to try to negotiate for a bigger slice of the Woods. She's the last wizard, and powerful. We need to convince her that the humans need more ground."

I had always thought that the Grand Mother was a legend. A story told to little children to frighten them. The only person more mythical than the Grand Mother was the Woodsman, and he definitely didn't exist. There was no magic in the human world. Once you left the safety of Vindolanda and entered the Woods, you had to contend with magic. But the only magic in the human news was the magic of werewolves, because they kept finding ways into the kingdom. Some new werewolves came from humans who had been seduced and bitten.

That a Grand Mother existed was news, but it made sense—the wizards had created the world as it was. There had to be a wizard lineage—an authority to stay neutral in the war. Or maybe they weren't neutral. After all, the humans had a crowded territory, and the werewolves had the Woods. They just went on.

As we walked in silence, I wondered how a warrior like Red would fare faced with a wizard. Red had no magic, just weapons. Who knew what a wizard could do?

"How are we going to find the Grand Mother?"

"That part's easy," answered Red.

"Easy? We're in the Woods, we could be attacked any minute, and you think we can find the Grand Mother. How?"

"Well, there's a reason you're on this journey with me, besides your good looks."

"Thanks."

"I have a heart stone."

"A heart stone?" I answered dumbly.

"A heart stone is the last of our magical artifacts, the rest were destroyed in the war."

"I thought humans weren't allowed magic."

"Well, we don't like magic, and we don't use it in Vindolanda. Certainly, we're not allowed new magic, but old magic can't be destroyed."

"So this is old magic."

"Very old magic."

"And what does this magic do?"

"It leads descendants of wizards to the wizarding conclave so they too can be trained."

I took this in. I finally said, "You're suggesting that I can help."

"Uh-huh."

"So I have wizarding blood."

"Uh-huh."

"How do you know that I have wizarding blood when I've never even heard of such a thing?"

"Because the heart stone sought you out when we were in Vindolanda. Now that we are outside the human enclave, the heart stone, wielded by you, will find the Grand Mother."

"Shit."

"You should feel honored," she said.

"I feel like a meal on legs."

"Well, that too."

"So you're my escort."

"I'm your chance to stay alive."

"And the likelihood of me sleeping in a bed tonight?" Maybe I didn't have to ask.

"You only run a six minute mile."

"Have you ever been to this place before?"

"No one born has been to this place before. First we had to find the heart stone in the archive and then we had to find you. You and I just have to survive the journey there and back."

"Great."

"It's time to contribute. You want to help, don't you?"

And I thought about Vindolanda. Vindolanda, the human enclave on the prairie. Its green fields, its crowded villages, the laughter of small children before they had been told of the wolves and the Woods. Fuck.

"Well, what do I have to do, exactly?"

"I'm sorry to say this is going to hurt."

She had turned to look at me. I was looking at her, and her eyes were full of pity.

"It's called the heart stone because it needs blood. We have to carve a space in your chest where the stone can rest."

"Doesn't blood attract werewolves?"

"Blood and light attract werewolves. The heart stone works by getting brighter as you move in the right direction."

"Great. So I'm going to be attracting werewolves."

"Yes. Here's a dagger. If we are attacked and I die, kill yourself."

I had to point out the obvious. "Why are we only two?"

"We didn't want to attract attention. No one can find out about our mission, and we can't scare off the Grand Mother by showing up in armored vehicles. We need her trust. A bleeding man and his guardian. That's an act of courage. Wizards appreciate that sort of bravado. Well, they're supposed to."

"I don't have a choice," I commented futilely.

"You don't have a choice. I've got the stone, a knife, and you don't know how to get back to the base or how to navigate in the Woods."

I took off my jacket and opened my shirt. She took a small vial out of her pocket. She smeared blue goo on my skin. It felt warm and then cool as my skin was numbed.

"This is all I can do for you," she said. "Want a gag? You can't scream. Screaming will attract attention."

"I want the gag."

She gagged me.

She looked at me, she reached out for my hand and held it, and with her other hand, she took the tip of her knife and drew it across my skin. I didn't feel anything at first, and then I felt an angry burning that quickly got more painful. I screamed soundlessly against my gag. When I thought I couldn't bear the carving into my flesh anymore, she took what looked like a dark piece of charcoal the size of a small plum and pushed it as gently as she could into my bleeding chest. The piece of charcoal drank my blood and started glowing red. It kept drinking my blood, sipping it. I felt the pain of the cut, the warmth of my blood seeping into the stone, and the stone warming slowly and shining. I realized I would not have to rely on the red light of the stone because part of the stone's magic was knowing, completely knowing, like I had never known anything before, where we needed to go.

"We need to take a left," I said.

"There's a fork in the next half hour or . . . "

That's when I first heard the sound of a werewolf. It was a strange sound. More than an animal sound. A magic sound. The sound of bones being crushed by stones mixed with the sound of raspy breathing by an enormous, angry, creature.

"I thought werewolves were supposed to be stealthy."

"They are; they normally circulate in the canopy. I've never heard this before. Must be the magic. Sometimes magic calls to magic."

I took my dagger. The heart stone, luckily, dimmed as the sound of the werewolf grew louder. I guess it wanted me alive.

Red looked around, made her way to the closest Old One and started climbing it. She hissed, "Come!"

And I scrambled over the thicket, trying to reach a branch. Thorns tore into me, my blood smearing the leaves. She leaned down from the branch and reached her hand out to me. I took it and tried to help but couldn't. She hoisted me up next to her. "Climb," she commanded.

I climbed. Reaching with my arms and pulling myself up hurt; it jostled the stone, but the stone held secure, sucking more of my blood the more efforts I made. It was an uncomfortable climb, but my desperation made me go fast.

Red followed me up a few feet, let me move away from her a few feet, drew her bow. I drew my dagger and looked around. The tree had long, fat branches, spread out in a fan at every level, and we could stand side by side, with room to maneuver.

The werewolf noise was growing louder.

"How many do you think there are?"

"I'm hoping just one. When there's more than one, it sounds like thunder racing towards you."

"How big are these things?"

"Big enough."

The noise had stopped. I realized I was holding my breath and was about to pass out.

"It must have cloaked."

"Cloaked?"

"They have magical cloaks. We're taught to look for inconsistencies at the edge of our vision. But they're essentially invisible."

The heart stone was glowing blue now. A low seeping blue, and in the blue light I saw a shape, a shimmering blue shape, taller than Red, broader than the two of us combined, with long, sharp claws.

Red saw it too. She took her bow, aimed and shot at the shape, which was moving fast when the arrow hit. The beast didn't make a sound. It just kept coming.

I was hyperventilating, and the blood stone's blue glow was growing more intense as the wolf approached.

Red stepped between us, sword and dagger drawn. The blue shape grabbed her by the throat, but she kept hacking at its arms and chest. If bones could laugh, that would be the sound I heard. I was growing weaker and the heart stone was growing bluer, and Red was hacking with her sword. But the beast was still advancing towards me when I felt a charge in my chest and a stream of blue light crackled out of me and hit the beast as I passed out.

I was pulled out of darkness by Red—she was shaking me and screaming. I couldn't make out her words. I felt numb and sick, and I wondered if we had died. Probably not because Red was bleeding and I could feel the heart stone drinking my blood faster.

"We have to go."

"Is it dead?" I asked, as I looked at the shape lying on the ground, a few feet away from me.

"No. I don't think so. Stunned, like you. I'll kill it, but then we have to go."

She took her sword, stabbed the beast's heart, and started whacking at the head. It took her a few minutes to cut off the head, black blood pooling around her feet, the wolf's eyes turning green and then fading to white. The wolf shape disappeared once the head was off, and a beautiful, headless, female body lay on the ground. The wolf's head, with its gnashing teeth, lay on one cheek next to the body.

I tried to stand and stumbled.

"The magic must be draining you."

"I can feel the stone drinking my blood faster now."

The stone was glowing, red and brighter, and I needed to go straight.

Straight followed a stream, where jumping fish glowed mauve in the moonlight, and I was reaching out my hand to touch one when Red grabbed me and spun me around.

"I should give you the standard warning. Those fish are enchanted. Their touch removes their weight in flesh. Writers need hands, usually."

"Ah."

So I kept walking, eyeing the fish with a leery gaze, still entranced by their moonlit dance. The stream went gently downriver and the bushes didn't grow quite so close to the stream. I was grateful for the easier walking now that I was too tired to run. The heart stone was wearing me out; my legs felt leaden and I didn't know how much farther we'd have to go, or if Red would end up carrying me.

A little bit before I couldn't bear any more, Red glanced my way and said, "You look terrible," and we stopped, mercifully.

We slept, which gave me some of my strength back. I felt like I had doubled in age, and my mood wasn't improved when we ate rations that tasted like rotten beans, which was close since they were fermented beans— energy food, Red called it, farting ahead of me.

Three days into the march, we heard a werewolf pass by and were relieved not to fight. But an hour later, the sound of rolling thunder made its way toward us.

"Shit," said Red.

"When you say it, I believe it," said I.

"They're coming. It will be more than one wolf this time. Try to stay out of the way. Or do that blue bolt thing again."

"I wish I knew how to make it happen, but I don't. It just . . . came out of me."

"Well, make it come again if you can."

"Are we climbing into the trees?"

"No point. We're just going to have to stand and fight. Dagger?"

"Dagger ready." I had a stranglehold on the dagger.

"Just remember, it's better if you die than if they catch you."

"I'm not forgetting."

The rolling thunder approached. I was nervous. Red had barely handled one wolf, how would she do with several? The only way I could help was to wait for magic I had no control over to manifest.

I gritted my teeth, clutched my dagger, and breathed, trying to focus on the heart stone, to see if I could exert any kind of control over it.

"How you doing back there?" she asked.

"Great."

"Feeling anything like a wizard?"

"Not much, thanks."

I felt my blood seeping into the stone, but I had grown used to that, and I felt the stone exhorting me to head northwest as fast as I could. My body was practically arguing with the stone, the stone's message was so urgent. I suddenly noticed that the rolling thunder sound had stopped.

"Damn, they've cloaked. Where are you?"

She looked straight at me and spun around as though she couldn't see me.

"I'm right here," I answered.

"Well, that's a new twist. You've disappeared. Keep doing that."

"No problem. I'll keep doing what I'm not doing."

"Now get out of the way so I don't slice you inadvertently. Why don't you go there"—she pointed at a tree we had passed a few feet back, and I retreated behind the trunk, still able to watch the fight.

I clutched the silvery smooth bark of an Old One, unable to see my hands. Red had retreated into a corner at the base of a tree. I guessed that this was so she couldn't be attacked from behind. She was suddenly lifted into the air, and instead of fighting it, she reached out one hand and found a grip, and knowing now where one body was, started stabbing the body of the werewolf that was grabbing her with her silver dagger. Very quickly, pools of blood hung in the air, making a vague outline of an upside down torso. She kept stabbing furiously when suddenly her body straightened out and I could tell that another werewolf had grabbed one of her legs because claw shaped gashes were appearing on her thighs. Red was kicking wildly and continuing to stab with her free hand. A werewolf body suddenly materialized and fell down the length of the tree, surrounded by a black cloak.

Red let go of the first werewolf and fell back to the ground, assuming a fighting stance. She was knocked back hard into the tree. She screamed. I was very nervous for her and didn't know what to do. So I took my dagger and approached the spot where I hoped the werewolf was. I stabbed the air until I made contact. I got lucky and shoved my knife into the base of its skull, which was clear when the second werewolf fell to the ground and I could see it, its cloak's power broken because the beast was dead at my feet.

"I can see you now. That was a little too close," said Red.

I nodded and kicked the wolf's body out of the way so I could help Red limp to a mossy trunk. We sat down, and I held her bag while she dug around it for field dressing supplies.

I looked at her. She looked at me. I had blood on my hands.

"We're starting to look ragged," she commented.

"Better ragged than dead."

"You're sounding more like a soldier. Thanks for helping out, by the way. That was quite brave."

"Not really. I was invisible. And I was lucky."

She nodded. And we sat, exhausted, staring at the ground for a while.

It was two more days of walking, and one more fight with a werewolf, much the same as the first, leaving me weaker than a newborn, but still able to walk in a stumbling fashion until we came to a meadow.

Red cooed, "Do you see those?"

Flowers. I was nonplussed. I had not seen flowers in the Woods. But here was a field of short pink flowers and tall-stemmed white flowers, and it was lovely, and it was unexpected.

And Red just kept saying, "I can't believe it."

"Flowers? You—you get super excited about flowers?"

"These aren't flowers, they're warders. They are a good omen. Were-wolves don't go anywhere near warders. At least that's the legend."

Which is when we saw a beautiful girl, dressed in leaves and moss, wearing a crown of flowers, halfway up a hill in front of us.

"I wonder if that's the wizard," said Red.

"I wonder if that's a werewolf," said I.

"You know werewolves are rarely human."

"Only when they want to mate and make new wolves."

"If you're right, and it would be creepy if you were because it would make you more paranoid than I am—well, we're surrounded by warders, and that should dampen the magic of the wolf."

My heart stone had grown cold. "Wait, I can't feel my heart stone, how am I supposed to find the wizard now?"

"Maybe we won't have to look any further."

"Your optimism worries me."

"I'll go talk to her, you sit down and rest. Pick some flowers; smell some flowers—they have healing properties."

I sat down. The flowers smelled sweet, like a young girl wearing her first perfume at a village ball. I started tucking the flowers into my clothes, pressing them into my chest like a balm. The heart stone kept cooling, and the torn flesh around the stone hurt less. I felt a little foolish, mashing the flowers against my skin, but the more I stuck to me, the better I felt.

In the field of warders my full exhaustion came upon me like a lead blanket surrounding my body. I watched Red approach the woman, and suddenly I felt frozen there in the field, flowers mashed into my chest, the smell surrounding me like a fog. The woman seemed nice at first, but suddenly there were several women with weapons surrounding Red. Red was fighting bravely, but she was surrounded and the situation looked hopeless.

I suddenly heard two voices behind me talking about me.

"You sure this is the one?" said an older sounding woman's voice.

"Yes, we've been following them. He has a heart stone in his chest," said a younger voice.

"The wizarding stone hasn't been seen in generations. This is a great day for werekind."

The old woman sounded excited. Their voices were coming closer. I didn't know what would happen next.

"Why is he so still?" asked the young one.

"The warders are well knows as healers and good omens, what's not often discussed is the unfortunate side effect of healing—a freezing effect which grows stronger in proportion to your need for the healing. He must have been very ill. The traditional use of warders is to cut them and bring them home, and administer them right before sleep. I guess our young wizard wasn't informed. You know the mission?"

"Yes, I know the mission, Wise One," said the younger voice, sounding deflated.

"Tell me again."

A strange sight stepped in front of my eyes. An old woman whose body was half wolf half woman—the wolf part starting at the waist. I had no idea this kind existed. She addressed me.

"I surprise you, young one. I am the oldest of the wolves. Age has few privileges, but in my case, I have partially mastered the turning. So you see me presently, half turned. Able to run like a wolf, but talk like a woman. Unsettling, eh?"

I would have gulped and nodded, if I had been able.

"You won't be able to speak for quite a while," she remarked, caressing my face. "Meet your mate," she said, turning to the woman besides her.

A tall, statuesque blonde gave me a cold, appraising look. She had green eyes, the color of new spring leaves, but there was something deeply dead about her gaze. Like a snake.

"I take this piece of meat to the Grand Mother, get past the protections into her house, and eat her whole for her powers."

"And?" probed the wolfwoman.

"I won't be able to kill for a week as I absorb her. Then I turn this one."

"We need two wizards to assure the next generation is born. That is the point. Don't disappoint me. I didn't spend ten months training you for nothing."

I was hoping I'd be killed soon, but apparently I was destined to sleep with the mean blonde.

"You know how valuable wizards are. Don't rough him up too much."

"Time to meet the Grand Mother," said the blonde one, hoisting me onto her back with ease. "She has been waiting for you."

I tried to speak back but couldn't.

I watched a fighting Red become smaller as we walked out of the field of warders into the Woods again. I couldn't do anything, and I'm not sure I would have known what to do. I felt like a baby, totally at the mercy of the wider world.

I started feeling desperate. It didn't matter who or what I was. I just wanted to be home safe in a place I understood, surrounded by people who had low expectations of me. I was tired of the Woods, tired of the magic, tired of the heart stone draining me. I was afraid I would never see

Red again. I didn't want to die in this frozen exhausted body. If I could have cried, I would have wept messy tears and howled as snot dripped down my face. I didn't care about the wizard. I didn't care about the quest. I was exhausted by the constant danger and the constant effort. *Leave me alone!* I screamed in my head to no avail. Once I calmed down, I took comfort in being carried. That was grim delight—not having to use my legs anymore.

After an hour or two of walking, we arrived at a little cottage. It was utterly unremarkable, except for being the first human home I'd seen in days. It sat in a very tidy clearing, a place where nature made human sense once again and had been ordered and tamed for the purposes of growing a splendid garden and vegetable patch. A vegetable patch which, now that I looked at it more attentively, contained plants I had never seen before.

About ten feet before the door, my carrier stopped and called out.

"Grand Mother! Grand Mother! I bring the next wizard with me. He bears the heart stone. Let us in."

I was the magic ticket into the Grand Mother's home? Now I felt mute and resentful. As soon as the Grand Mother looked at me, I hoped my eyes could convey my worry. I wasn't sure what to expect, and then I heard the shuffling step of an elderly person. Suddenly I was looking at the forehead of a perfectly ordinary looking old woman. Not even my eyes could move. That was annoying too.

The Grand Mother pinched my cheek and said, "You're in a bad shape, boy. Thank God you found some warders to keep you alive when you did. Otherwise you would have been dead before reaching my door, by the looks of you. Let's see what we can do to improve this sorry situation. I'm glad to meet you, Apprentice."

I had no intention of learning magic. I wanted to get away from the evil blonde and have a long hot soak in a bath. That was the limit of my ambition.

"It's a good thing this young lady brought you to me. If the wolves had found you it would have been a disaster. They would have taken you hostage and used your blood for their magic. What is your name?" She had turned to the blonde.

"Lilith. It was a hard journey here. He told me where to go before he went mute. I brought some warders to heal our wounds. We've been in several fights."

The Grand Mother stopped, made an intricate hand gesture and there was a sound, like the parting of theatre curtains, and we shuffled forth into the cottage. It was strangely old fashioned, tidy but crowded with arcane objects I assumed had some purpose—skulls, feathers, stones, jars with potions. The fireplace had a great fire and two iron hooks supporting a large iron pot.

"Are you hungry? Let me get you something to eat and drink. Oh, I'll have to help this young man out. I can't undo the freeze, but I can help him so he can swallow the food." She rubbed her hands against a golden amber globe, and then touched my throat with her thumbs. I could swallow, and I tried to move my lips, but found I still couldn't speak or move my body.

She served us stew from the fireplace, which was earthy tasting, like mushrooms and roots, and delicious, flavored with herbs I couldn't quite identify. The blonde was surprisingly gentle in slowly feeding me. I ate to my heart's content. Eating hot food had grown strangely foreign—it seemed all too human. I had become used to my cold bean diet in very little time. I was getting drowsy sitting by the warm fire, sipping strong sweet tea and eating stew.

"I know I don't carry the heart stone," the blonde said to the woman, "but I too want to be your apprentice."

"That's a lot to ask. Those that don't have the blood find it exceedingly difficult. It takes them ten times longer to learn a fraction of the knowledge, and their magic is unreliable at best."

"You must be able to teach me something?"

"Not much, a few arcane arts like weather and palm reading. Sometimes a little fortune telling through tea leaves. Some basic healing potions, but that's closer to medicine."

"Grand Mother, I hope you'll allow me to rest for a few days before I start my journey back."

"Of course, rest as you need, and I will do what I can to help you regain your strength."

"Could I ask for one magical favor?"

The Grand Mother stiffened. "You can ask. I will decide on the wisdom of the request."

"I would like the luck spell cast."

"That's a hard one—I will need to prepare. But I am willing."

"Thank you, Grand Mother. Let me know if I can help."

The Grand Mother started shuffling around the house, pulling ingredients off shelves, muttering to herself, sometimes smiling, sometimes scowling. She mixed ingredients in a bowl and set the potion afire with a green flame, and a familiar smell filled the house—that of oranges and cloves.

"That is the smell of luck," said the Grand Mother.

"That's it?" said the blonde.

"Not quite. Now I need to pray for the potion to reabsorb the luck."

She sat down and started chanting softly. Her eyes turned white and wisps of light started swirling around her. She stopped talking and seemed oblivious to us.

The blonde got up suddenly, walked over to me, picked me up, and lay me on a cot. I had no idea why. She then walked over to a purple egg sitting on a shelf. She cracked it open into her mouth. She walked up behind the white-eyed Grand Mother, and then the strangest thing I had ever seen happened. The blonde's head started to swell and grow, stretching as she opened her mouth wide. She leaned over the Grand Mother, who remained oblivious to what was happening around her. The blonde slowly but surely swallowed the Grand Mother whole. And then sat down, looking unnaturally pregnant and distorted, like a human reptile. She burped loudly. I stared, horrified, as she started aging rapidly.

"I know I'm getting older. I can feel my joints creaking. Side effect of eating the truly old. Luckily, once I have absorbed the Grand Mother's magic, I can heal myself. No need to panic. You won't be sleeping with a crone."

Her hair was growing grey and getting long, even coming out of her ears and covering her nose. Her nails were yellowing, thickening, and growing into long, sharp claws.

"It's never been tried before," she commented. "We weren't sure how the wereblood and the magic would come together. As I learn to control this, I'll look more human. Just another reason why I'm covered in warders to suppress the wolf, she said, winking and pointing to her skirt, which had split open to reveal a woven web of flowers beneath it. That's why her magic alarms didn't sound when I came to her door. Neat, eh? I'm going to need to rest now. You rest too."

I did. I slept deeply, though my dreams were filled with visions of Red screaming out as she was hacked to death by a circle of young women with bloodlust in their eyes.

For two days I lay on the bed and watched my now immobile, aged blonde, sleep.

I then started hearing screaming. A loud male voice, the familiar sound of Red, and the sound of several other female voices. A fight was coming closer to the Grand Mother's house. I was thrilled to know Red was alive, and wondering whether she had the strength left to stay alive. I hoped so. I didn't know what could be done about the sleeping digesting wolf on the floor.

Someone kicked in the door and a giant man's head appeared. A Woodsman, immense, just like the legends. Besides wizards, these were the rarest of the enchanted people. They too were of the woods but were rarely seen. They tended the trees in magic groves. And they were allied with wizards.

"I came as soon as I felt the Grand Mother's energy seep out of the forest," said the low, gravelly voice of the giant man. He had to enter the cottage by crouching and couldn't stand once inside.

He saw the giant mass I had been staring at on the floor. He said, "It's only been two days. Maybe we're still lucky." He took out his knife.

Red came in after him, covered in blood, her clothes ripped and muddied.

"He saved my life," she said, as she came to sit next to me.

The Woodsman was very gently, very carefully, cutting the belly of the blonde. There was no blood in the cut; the body was sliced open cleanly. The tiny head of the Grand Mother slowly emerged, then her body, which had shrunk. As soon as her hands were free, she started an incantation and golden lights started swirling around her. As she grew, the body of the blonde simultaneously deflated around her feet, until all that was left was a bag of skin. And the Grand Mother was whole.

"Thank you, Woodsman," said the Grand Mother.

"I'm just glad you're still whole," said the Woodsman.

"She absorbed much of my magic, but not enough to stop me healing myself once her spell was broken by your knife."

I was blinking.

"How are you feeling?" asked Red, turning to me.

"Much better," I said, surprised I could speak.

The Woodsman came over to me and said, "I can help you." He rubbed his hand over my chest. Very suddenly the heart stone turned cold, my flesh healed, and the stone just popped out, landing on my chest, where it was plucked by the Woodsman.

Red smiled and said, "They are great healers."

The Woodsman gave the stone to Red and said, "Now you."

And he placed his hand on the claw wounds on her thighs and the knife wounds on her face, arms and chest, and she too closed up, the blood disappearing under his touch.

"Now good night," said the Woodsman, "I must get back to my groves. I look forward to seeing the Apprentice under other circumstances," he said. I nodded, confused. "Goodbye, Grand Mother."

"Goodbye, Woodsman."

And he left, majestically and quietly, crouching on his way out of the cottage, and then disappearing into the Woods.

"What is your name?" asked the Grand Mother of Red.

"My name is Red."

"I have a gift for you," said the Grand Mother. And she went to a small trunk and pulled out a cloak. "Try this on," she said. And the cloak, which had been black, changed colors as soon as Red touched it.

"I'm giving you the first invisibility cloak for humans. I've been working on it for some time now."

Red pulled it around her shoulders, the red fabric glowed for a moment, and she promptly disappeared.

THE END

Dear Josephine Stone,

When you died on October 28, 2011, at the tender age of twenty-three, we lost a talented writer, enthusiastic managing editor, and dear friend. A shining star fell from the sky over Richmond, Virginia, that night. Then Destiny pinned it back to the velvet curtains, and Oderus Urungus's voice boomed, "You better give Josie everything she ever wanted." And since we knew you always wanted a book, we gave you one. Actually, we gave you two—*The Nest: An Anthology of The Real* and *Airborne: An Anthology of The Unreal.*

We dedicate both anthologies to you, wishing that they do justice to your creative gifts, aspirations, and memory. For your sake, we hope that death is better than life, but, as Tristan told Isolde, love is more than both. We love you, Josie.

Feathery hugs,

The Quail Bell Crew

ABOUT THE EDITORS

Jade Miller is a 2011 graduate of Virginia Commonwealth University. Shortly after graduating from VCU, she served as an assistant editor at *Quail Bell Magazine*. Now she studies education at the University of Richmond, aspiring to one day teach English to gifted high school students.

Christine Stoddard is a 2012 graduate of Virginia Commonwealth University. She founded *Quail Bell Magazine* in 2010. Now she runs Quail Bell Press & Productions, LLC, and writes full-time. Christine lives in Richmond, Virginia, with her sister.